To Sister Donna:
God Bless!
[signature]
10/08/05

TALL DRUMS

Portraits of Nigerians Who are Changing America

OTHER WORKS BY UGORJI O. UGORJI

The Crow Bride, and Other Torti Tales
From the Belly of the Gods
The Adventures of Torti: Tales From West Africa

TALL DRUMS

Portraits of Nigerians Who are Changing America

Ugorji Okechukwu Ugorji

A SUNGAI BOOK
Princeton, New Jersey
Owerri, Nigeria

SUNGAI

Tall Drums: Portraits of Nigerians Who are Changing America

A SUNGAI BOOK
Published by Sungai Corp.
P. O. Box 3295
Princeton, New Jersey 08543-3295

Copyright © Ugorji O. Ugorji, 1998

First Printing, 2002; Second Printing 2004

All rights reserved. No part of this publication may be reproduced, transmitted or stored in a retrieval system in any form or by any means electronic or mechanical or otherwise, without the written permission of the author and publisher.

All requests for permission, and inquiries regarding rights should be mailed to:
Sungai Corp.
P. O. Box 3295, Princeton, New Jersey 08543-3295

Cover Design and Book Formatting by Dilip Kane

Library of Congress Control Number: 98-060017

ISBN: 1889218-14-6 Clothe

Note: The photographs on Pages 1 and 15 are those of Tim Robinson of the Timbuktu Dancers and Drummers, Trenton, New Jersey, taken by Amaka Eze, 1999.

DEDICATION

To African Americans who paved the way for Nigerians in America, with blood, tears, sweat, love, and a legacy of struggle that has been transformational and prophetic. And specifically to Molifi Kete Asante, Donald Kofi Tucker, and the late Joseph Nanven Garba.

Tall Drums

Photo by Marvin Ross, 2002.

The drum remains a necessary and powerful tool of communication and celebration among Nigerians, even in the United States. Above, drummers announce the arrival of Vice President Atiku Abubakar, GCON of Nigeria at a reception for him, on July 26, 2002, in Trenton, New Jersey.

TABLE Of CONTENTS

Dedication	iv
Acknowledgements	ix
Preface	xi
PART ONE: OFFICIAL NIGERIA	**1**
Professor Jibril Aminu	2
Chief Arthur Mbanefo	6
Honorable Joseph Chiedu Keshi	10
Mr. Taofiq Olawale Oseni	12
PART TWO: FEATURED PORTRAITS	**15**
Alash'le G. Abimiku	16
Chinua Achebe	20
Vincent I. Ahonkhai	24
Babatunde Junaid Ayeni	28
Callista O. Chukwunenye	32
Pius J. Egbelu	36
Theophilus O. Egbujor	40
Azubuike L. Ezeife	44

TABLE Of CONTENTS Continued

Philip C. Emeagwali	48
Oloruntoyin O. Falola	52
Alfred Olusegun Fayemi	56
Ibrahim A. Gambari	60
Joseph Nanven Garba	64
John Kalu Ijem	68
Michael N. C. Mbabuike	72
Chike Momah	76
Obioma Nnaemeka	80
Bartholomew O. Nnaji	84
John Nwangwu	88
Daniel Chinedu Nwankwo	92
James Esomonu Obi	96
Elizabeth Odilile Ofili	100
Emmanuel W. Onunwor	104
Charles Chibuike Onyirimba	108
Steven Adekunle Osunsami	112
Juliette Modupe Tuakli	116
Henrietta Ngozi Ukwu	120

ACKNOWLEDGEMENTS

In 1996 the first set of letters went out to Nigerian organizations and distinguished professionals I knew in the Nigerian community across the US announcing my plans for **Tall Drums**, and calling for nominations. As the nominations came, I was faced with the difficulty of selecting from so many people, based on some relative objectivity. I called on Dr. Chinyere Egbe, who is now the Dean of the School of Business Administration at Medgar Evers College, City University of New York, to help me with the selections. Using a set of criteria he and I put together, Dr. Egbe went through the nominees at the time and made recommendations. While some others have been added to his recommendations, I am grateful to him for the advice and guidance he provided. He did so knowing that his role in the selection process would eliminate him from among those profiled in this volume of **Tall Drums**.

Following the selections, I began the process of contacting those nominated, for interviews and for permission to tell their stories, albeit in the limited fashion I have done in this work. I thank all of those profiled here, for their time and kindness, and for taking me seriously enough to believe in the value of the effort. I also thank the various people who took the various photographs of those profiled (see the photo credits) for granting me and the Sungai Corporation permission to use the images in this book.

Over the years I have enjoyed the constituency services of Ambassadors, and Consul Generals of Nigeria, in Washington, DC, in New York, and in Atlanta, Georgia, as well as the assistance of various employees at these foreign service posts of Nigeria. I am grateful to Ambassador Jibril Aminu, Nigeria's current Ambassador to the United States, Ambassador Arthur Mbanefo, Nigeria's current Ambassador to the United Nations, Ambassador Joe Keshi, Consul General of Nigeria in Atlanta, and Mr. Taofiq Oseni - the man whom Chika Oyeani once called the "people's consul general"- Consul General of Nigeria in New York. Before these men, the eminent Ambassador Ibrahim Gambari (to the UN), Ambassador Hassan Adamu (to the USA), and Mr. Awani, the former Consul General of Nigeria in New York, were supportive and appreciative of the efforts at Sungai Corporation to document and propagate the creative and intellectual products of African people in book form.

I received some of the photographs in this book from the Nigerian Embassy in Washington, DC, from the Nigerian House in New York, and from the Office of the Consulate

General of Nigeria in Atlanta. I am grateful to Mrs. Elizabeth Oddiri, Head of the Information Department at the Office of the Consulate General in New York, her deputy, Mr. Nura Ishak, Mr. Tanko Suileman, Special Assistant to Nigeria's Ambassador to the United Nations, Dr. Ozichi Alimole, Head of the Commerce Department at the New York Office of the Consulate General, and Mr. Sada Soli Jibiya, Special Assistant to the Nigerian Ambassador to the US, for their assistance in obtaining photographs and certain information. I also thank the editors and photographers at the *African Quest,* an Africa-oriented newspaper in Atlanta, Georgia, for some of the photographs.

For over ten years that I have known him, Mr. Dilip Kane has provided such stellar consulting services in design and formatting for Sungai Books; I thank him for this one. I also acknowledge with thanks the assistance of 'Damola Ifaturoti in scanning some of the photographs, as well as Dr. Marie Umeh's editiong services.

PREFACE

African peoples had been in the U.S. long before the American revolution, voluntarily and involuntarily, including those whose origins were in the geographical area that became known as Nigeria in 1914 under British occupation. The more contemporary immigrants to the U.S. from this part of Africa came as students, scholars, and even entrepreneurs. Inspired by the Black struggle in America and seeking to cash-in on the freedom rhetoric of Britain and America during the Second World War, some of these Nigerian immigrants would eventually return home to foment and lead the movements for national independence in the 1940s and 1950s. Most prominent among these Nigerians was Dr. Nnamdi Azikiwe, who would later be known as the father of the independent Nigerian nation, following its independence in 1960. "Zik of Africa," as he was popularly known, served as the nation's first African Governor General, and later as its first President until 1966. He was an alumnus of Lincoln University in Pennsylvania.

When *Tall Drums* was conceived in 1996, a military junta held sway in the affairs of government in Nigeria. An armada of human rights activists and democracy advocates, led by the likes of Olisa Agbakoba (SAN) and Gani Fawehinmi (SAN), had sprung up in a long and sustained struggle to force a return to civilian rule. The advance fee (419) scam, and the highly publicized incidents of drug trafficking by a few Nigerians, had turned the once honored and glorious name of Nigeria to a badge of shame, with millions of its outstanding citizens all over the world subjected to embarrassing national-origin-profiling at major international ports. Gradually and sadly, citizens of a nation who were once sought after as visitors and residents all over the world, became pariahs in the global village.

That image was strange and painful for me. It was strange because none of the Nigerian men and women I knew in my professional and social circles fit the profile that the international media had projected. And it was painful because I became, as many associates of mine were, lumped into one stereotype of the scamming and corrupt Nigerian, which belied the true facts of the quiet, progressive revolution that African people of Nigerian nationality were masterminding in numerous professions globally. *Tall Drums* was conceived to paint a different picture, a more accurate portrait of perhaps the most hardworking people in the world.

I chose to look within the United States of America because it is where I have been fortunate and grateful to reside for the past 20 years. I sought to identify Nigerians, who are, for me, an indispensable part of the quilt of Africa's (and yes, humanity's) promise. My aim was to produce a book that would educate the reader, as well as recast the Nigerian in a more positive and factual image. I confess that this is not a "balanced" picture of the presence of Nigerians in America. I deliberately skew the image scale toward some of the brightest and most accomplished because the image pendulum had swung so unfairly in the other direction. And while the notion of "changing America" might appear hyperbolic, it is truly my belief that each of these men and women has changed America somehow, for some people, or for someone.

It is estimated that about one million Nigerians currently reside in the United States legally. While Nigerian immigrants are resident in every state of the Union, there are pockets of high concentration around the major urban centers in America. In the Northeast, which is the entry region for over 75% of Nigerian immigrants, significant populations of Nigerians (in the tens of thousands) can be found in New York and its boroughs, in Newark or in the Essex County area of New Jersey, in Philadelphia, Pennsylvania, in Baltimore, Maryland, and in the nation's capital city of Washington, DC. In the Southern part of the US where the weather and environment approximates the Nigerian urban terrain, Nigerians can be found in astonishing numbers in Atlanta, Georgia, Houston and Dallas, Texas, in Nashville, Tennessee, and in the State of Florida. In the West Coast, Nigerians can be found in significant numbers in various cities, including Los Angeles, California.

According to Tim Borke of the Carnegie Endorwment for International Peace, Nigerians have the highest average level of educational attainment of all immigrant groups in the United States, with the average Nigerian immigrant holding at least a Bachelor's degree. The reason for this level of education is partially rooted in the fact that the Nigerians who migrated to the U.S. before the 1990s, were generally those from relatively well-off families and/or those sponsored by Federal and State governments to gain certain expertise in American institutions. Nigerian tertiary institutions were not enough and did not have adequate room for all the qualified high school graduates and other professionals who sought to continue with their education. The trend at that time was that these educational refugees returned home after their studies to take up positions in various sectors of the developing nation's economy and administration. Even the entrepreneurs among them came, transacted their businesses within weeks, and left. As such, there was little or no interest on the part of Nigerian immigrants to seek U.S. citizenship. All of that changed, starting from the late 1980s. Political instability occasioned by military coups, mismanagement in several quarters, and global economic trends turned the oil-fueled prosperity of Nigeria into a nightmare. Consequently, many of its citizens, for the second time in Nigeria's post independence history, became economic and political refugees.

Since the 1990s, the average Nigerian immigrant to the U.S. no longer looks to rush home after studies or business. Economic activities rather than education have become the major reason for migration. They began to seek permanent residency and U.S. citi-

Portraits of Nigerians Who are Changing America

zenship in numbers that were unheard of. And the well-off among them began to not just buy homes, but some have erected the kinds of mansions in some of the suburbs of America that suggests that they have decided to settle. Accompanied with this new settlement mindset is the Nigerian community's zeal to organize its members, particularly along social, cultural, and ethnic axis. These organizations have tended to form around local and state dimensions in various parts of the U.S., but in 1990s, three major ethnic organizations with reach across the U.S. sprung up. They are the World Igbo Congress, which has affiliate Igbo unions in various U.S. cities and beyond; the Egbe Omo Yoruba, with Yoruba affiliates across the country; and Zumunta, which is largely composed of Nigerians from the North (Hausa, Fulani, and others), with affiliates also across the U.S. There is also Movement for the Survival of Ogoni People (MOSOP) which has organizational presence in the US, and many other ethnically based organizations. But more recently, two attempts have been made at the Nigerian federal level to organize the community as a unit in America. The two groups that are making the efforts are the Nigerian Peoples Forum (NPF), and the Nigerians in the Diaspora Organization (NIDO), both of which are headquartered in Washington, DC.

Academe is one area where Nigerians have found a strong foothold in America, in fields ranging from African Studies to Robotics Engineering. Many have risen to positions as Deans of Schools, Chairperson of Departments, and occupants of endowed chairs in many of the most prestigious institutions in the country. Notable among them are Bart Nnaji at the University of Pittsburgh, Pennsylvania, Toyin Falola at the University of Texas at Austin, Texas, and Chinua Achebe at Bard College, New York. In politics, Nigerians have been appointed or have won elections to school boards in New Jersey (Ugorji Ugorji in Trenton, and Elliot Isibor in Irvington), appointed Secretary of Health in Florida (Dr. John Agwunobi), appointed as City Treasurer in Philadelphia, Pennsylvania (Folaside Olanitekun), and elected as Mayor in East Cleveland, Ohio (Emmanuel Onunwor). In the arts, the legendary drummer Babatunde Olatunji, the film maker Tony Abulu, the singer Floxy-Bee, the masqueraded and Abigbo dancer, Mike Mbagwu, and the novelist Chudi Uwazurike, among many others, continue to thrill Nigerians and Americans alike with their creative energies. In computer science and artificial intelligence, Phillip Emeagwali continues to raise the bar with speed and innovation. In the media, ABC's Steve Osunsami, CNN's Chiaka Okwu, USAfricaonline's Chido Nwangwu, *Nigeria & Africa's* Tesy Obioha, *African Herald's* Richard Nwachukwu, *African Quest's* Charles Onyirimba, Image Dynamics' Yinka Adeyemi, and *African Sun Time's* Chika Onyeani, continue to represent, as the Americans would say.

Even in such American sports preserves as basketball, and football, Nigerians, such as Hakeem Olajunwa, and Christian Okoye, respectively, have made their marks as champions. In boxing, not only did the legendary Dick Tiger of Nigeria win some of his most exciting championship bouts here, the likes of Henry Akinwande who now trains in the U.S. and Ike Ibeabuchi, have made their marks in American rings. And of course it was here, at the 1996 Atlanta Games, that Nigerians won their first Olympic gold medals in any sport. Chioma Ajunwa dethroned the American and World Long Jump queen, Jackie

Joyner Kousie, to capture the gold medal in the event. And oh, those members of the Nigerian men's football squad - they simply wrote and played symphonies with their feet and heads, and the Americans called it soccer, as the world showered them with gold medals.

Nonetheless, this book is being published at a time when much more than the image of Nigeria and Nigerians are at stake. The very continued existence of the nation as one unit is now loudly questioned at home and abroad. This question, however, is not new. It has been around since the amalgamation of the then northern and southern protectorates in 1914. Leading up to independence from Britain in 1960, it was Northern Nigeria, led mainly by the Hausa and Fulani, that first questioned the rush to independence and the wisdom of a nation called Nigeria as it was conceived. The loudest, most serious and most costly challenge came in the period between 1966 and 1970 when unfortunate events moved the then Eastern Nigeria, led mainly by the Igbo, to proclaim the short-lived Republic of Biafra. The war that ensued lasted for 30 months, with the demise of Biafra in January of 1970 and the loss of over one million lives. Virtually every one of Nigeria's 250-plus ethnic groups lost people in that skirmish that is now Africa's most forgotten nasty war, but the brunt of the war was borne mainly by the Igbo and other ethnic groups in the then Eastern Nigeria. By 1993, following the annulment of the presidential election believed to have been won by the late business mogul Moshood Abiola, it was the Yoruba's turn to call for separation as the solution to a perceived Northern-Islamic hegemony. And the wailing of ethnic minorities, ranging from the Tiv and the Jukun in the Middle Belt, to the Ogoni in the Delta region, continue to challenge the nation to negotiate a more perfect federation.

This writer shares the grand unifying vision of Zik, and the intellectual centering enterprise of Cheikh Anta Diop and Molefi Kete Asante. In a global village where the very humanity of the African has been denied and subjugated, the entity called Nigeria has been and remains the only serious modern sovereignty with the resources and resolve to defend and project the progenitors of the human family. Perhaps no other modern African nation (in fact, no other nation in the world) has sacrificed as much for the liberation and self-determination of African people than Nigeria. And this, Nigerians have done even with the paralysis of endemic mismanagement, inter-ethnic strife and religious uprisings that have plagued the young nation in its still infant years of 42. Imagine then what Nigeria could do, conjure what the nation and its "tall drums" could become, with effective and efficient leadership, in a sovereignty whose very structure and character are negotiated freely and willingly by all the constituting ethnic groups, big and small.

It has taken over four years to find the people profiled in this book and get them to take time off their schedules to speak with me. It was even harder to get photographs of them for a work I insisted must be of a coffee table format. Two of those profiled, Dr. Daniel Nwankwo, and General Joe Garba passed away before the publishing of this book. With the knowledge of their lovely widows, I decided to leave them in the book anyway, as perhaps my personal last tribute to their gentle souls. Those profiled are placed in alphabetical order by their last names. I have also interspersed among the pages of this book, photographs of Nigerians (not necessarily profiled) at various events and gatherings in the United States. These additional pictures are intended to show as much as can be gathered by the eyes, the motif, ethos, rituals, and politics that manifest in the diverse cultures of Nigerians in America. This work is not exhaustive by any means. All errors and omissions are mine. It is my hope that in subsequent volumes, the reach would be expanded.

Tall Drums

Photo by Marvin Ross, 2002.

Vice President Atiku Abubakar, GCON (left) is being welcomed to Trenton, New Jersey, by His Excellency Professor Ibrahim Gambari (in the middle), and Mr. Taofiq Oseni, Consular General of Nigeria, New York (right). Abubakar was in Trenton on July 26, 2002 to receive the 2002 Quintessence Award for "Distinguished accomplishments in public administration, and outstanding contributions to the history and heritage of African people." Gambari, who is the United Nations Under Secretary General and Special Adviser for Africa, chaired the occasion. The Quintessence Award is the premier Pan-African leadership award organized and presented each year by the New Jersey-based publishing and consulting firm, Sungai Corp.

Portraits of Nigerians Who are Changing America

PART ONE:

Photo by Sungai Corp. 1999.

Official Nigeria...

H. E. PROFESSOR JIBRIL AMINU

Nigeria's Ambassador to the United States of America

The career of His Excellency Professor Jibril Aminu has spanned the gamut of Nigeria's public space, with services as a distinguished physician, a towering academic, and as a consummate public administrator of international renown. Appointed by President Olusegun Obasenjo in 1999 to his current position as Ambassador of Nigeria to the United States, he is holding perhaps the premier ambassadorial post in Nigeria's foreign service. It has been his duty to sell to the Americans the new order in Nigeria since the nation returned to civilian government on May 29, 1999. He is now in his third year of shepherding Nigeria's relations with the world's only remaining superpower.

THE EARLY YEARS

Ambassador Aminu was born on August 25, 1939, in Song, Adamawa State. His elementary education took place at Song and at Yola, both in Adamawa. For his secondary education, he proceeded to the then Government College (now Barewa College), Zaria and graduated with distinction in 1957. Three years later, he obtained the General Certificate of Education (Advanced Level), also with distinction. His medical studies started at the then University College (Now University of Ibadan) London, and by 1965, he had obtained his medical degree. At his graduation, he was honored as the Best Medical Graduate that year, and awarded Gold Medals for Best Overall Performance in Community Health Pathology and Surgery. He completed postgraduate studies in medicine under the Commonwealth Scholars Program, at the Middlesex Hospital, The Royal London Hospital, and the Royal Post-Graduate Medical School, all in London.

CAREER DEVELOPMENTS

An internist, with specialization in cardiology, Ambassador Aminu started his medical career as a Senior House Officer at the University College Hospital, Ibadan in 1966. Following his post-graduate studies in London, he returned to Nigeria in 1972 to serve the North Eastern State government in the immediate postwar era of Nigeria. From 1973 to 1975, he served as a consultant to the University of Ibadan, and as a Senior Lecturer at the university's medical school. In 1975, he was appointed the Executive Secretary of the

Portraits of Nigerians Who are Changing America

His Excellency Professor Jibril Aminu

Photo courtesy of the Nigerian Embassy, Washington, D.C.

National Universities' Commission, a position in which he oversaw the planning, development, and budgets of all the institutions of higher education in Nigeria.

In 1979, Ambassador Aminu spent a year in the United States as a Visiting Professor at Howard University College of Medicine, Washington, DC. A year later, the then President of Nigeria, Alhaji Shehu Shagari, appointed him the Vice Chancellor of the University of Maiduguri, where he held a tenured position as a Full Professor of Medicine. During his tenure as Vice Chancellor, he initiated and supervised the establishment of the University of Maiduguri Teaching Hospital (UMTH). Following the return of the military to government, the eminent scholar was appointed Federal Minister of Education in 1985, a position in which he supervised the entire educational enterprise in Nigeria. Four years later, he was appointed to the sensitive position of Minister of Petroleum and Mineral Resources, in which he managed the sector that yields over 90% of the nation's revenues. During his tenure as Minister of Petroleum and Mineral Resources, he served as President of the African Petroleum Producers' Association (APPA) in 1991, and subsequently as President of the Organization of Petroleum Exporting Countries' Conference until 1992.

During the 1994 Constitutional Conference that was part of the national negotiation for a more perfect federation, Aminu was elected and he served as a Delegate from his constituency in Adamawa State. After the conference, he proceeded to become a Foundation Member, and a Trustee of the now ruling Peoples Democratic Party (PDP).

Ambassador Aminu is both a Member, and a Fellow of the Royal College of Physicians, London; a Fellow of the West African College of Physicians, a Foundation Fellow of the Nigerian Postgraduate Medical College; the only non-mathematician Fellow of the Mathematical Association of Nigeria; a Foundation Member of the African Academy of Sciences; a Member of the Nigerian Institute of Management; and a Fellow of the Nigerian Academy of Education, to mention just a few. He holds honorary doctorate degrees from Ahmadu Bello University, Zaria, and the Federal University of Technology, Yola.

Portraits of Nigerians Who are Changing America

Ambassador Aminu (center) joined President Bush and other ambassadors from various countries, in an event that marked six months since the September 11, 2001 attack on America.

H. E. ARTHUR C. I. MBANEFO

Ambassador & Permanent Representative of Nigeria to the United Nations

His Excellency, Chief Arthur Christopher Izuegbunam Mbanefo holds the regal status of *Odu of Onitsha*, the third citizen of the historic city of Onitsha in Anambra State. His title is three levels above the title held by the legendary father of the Nigerian nation, late Dr. Nnamdi Azikiwe, the Owelle of Onitsha. At the age of 70, Chief Mbanefo jettisoned a much deserved retirement to help President Olusegun Obasenjo usher in a new phase in Nigeria's march to greatness. He was appointed in 1999 as the Permanent Representative and Ambassador of Nigeria to the United Nations, a position he currently holds with characteristic resolve and patriotic fervor.

Born on June 11, 1930, Ambassador Mbanefo had his early education in Nigeria and England. Following his certification in England as an accountant, he received post-qualification training in the United States, where he worked with Coopers & Lybrand, and later with the management consulting firm of Price Waterhouse & Company in England.

CAREER DEVELOPMENTS

Ambassador Mbanefo's earliest marks in the history of Nigeria and Africa were made in the field of accounting. After his training in England, he returned to Nigeria in 1962 and joined the Lagos-based Akintola Williams & Company, the largest indigenous (Black-owned) professional firm of chartered accountants in the world - the firm is affiliated with Deloite Touche Tohmatsu International. He was made a full partner in the firm within only three years of employment, and remained a partner for over 21 years before founding his own firm of Arthur Mbanefo & Associates in 1986.

An international leader in his field, Ambassador Mbanefo served as a Board member of the International Accounting Standards Committee (IASC), and a Council member of the International Federation of Accountants (IFAC). He was instrumental in the establishment of the Association of Accountancy Bodies in West Africa, and served as the organization's President in 1987. He also served as the President of the Nigerian Association of Management Consultants (NAMCON) for three years. He is a fellow of the Institute of Chartered Accountants of Nigeria, the Chartered Institute of Accountants in England and Wales, and the Nigerian Institute of Management. Mbanefo designed and installed the first account-

Portraits of Nigerians Who are Changing America

His Excellency Chief Arthur C. I. Mbanefo, Odu of Onitsha

Photo courtesy of the Nigerian Permanent Mission to the United Nations, New York

ing system for the Nigerian Oil and Gas sectors. And for his contributions to the field, the Institute of Chartered Accountants of Nigeria awarded him its Gold Medal in 1996.

A trusted advisor to some of Nigeria's governments, Ambassador Mbanefo has been a key actor in many of Nigeria's nation building dramas. During the brief existence of Biafra, he was Biafra's Minister of Commerce and Industries. A consummate statesman, Mbanefo has served as the Pro-Chancellor of three of Nigeria's premier institutions of higher education, namely University of Lagos, Obafemi Awolowo University, and Ahmadu Bello University. Perhaps no man or woman understands Nigeria's contemporary divides more comprehensively than Mbanefo. His responsibilities as the Chairman of the nation's State Creation/Local Government, and Boundaries Adjustment Committee from 1995 to 1996, required him to travel the length and breadth of Nigeria, listening to, documenting, and making judgements on the citizens' grievances and agitation.

For his services, Nigeria and indeed other nations, have shown appreciation in the form of very high civilian honors. His awards include the Order of the Federal Republic of Nigeria, Commander of the Order of Merit of the Italian Republic, and Grand Officer of the National Order of the Southern Cross of Brazil. On May 13, 2000, Ambassador Mbanefo received the Princeton, New Jersey based Sungai Corporation's *Quintessence Award* for "outstanding services in Nigeria's nation building, and for contributions to the history and heritage of African people."

Portraits of Nigerians Who are Changing America

Ambassador Mbanefo (right) at a Sungai book launching in Newark, New Jersey, 2000.

Ambassador Mbanefo (center) shares the dais with Professor Chinua Achebe (seated left) and Dr. (Iddi) Ambrose Mgbako (seated right) at a Sungai book launching of a book by Chike Momah. Standing are Dr. (Mrs.) Christie Achebe (left) and Mr. and Mrs. Chike Momah.

JOSEPH CHIEDU KESHI

Consul-General of Nigeria, Atlanta, Ga.

The Honorable Joseph Cheidu Keshi came to the Atlanta outpost of Nigeria's Foreign Affairs in 1999. He was born on December 6, 1949 in Zaria, Kaduna State. His primary and secondary education took place in the historic city of Ibadan, where he attended St. Patrick's College, and later Loyola College. He holds a Bachelor's degree in Political Science from the University of Ibadan, and a Master's degree in administration and development from the Netherlands' Institute of Social Studies, the Hague, with special emphasis on policy analysis. He also holds a Diploma in International Relations and Diplomacy from the Nigeria Institute of International of International Affairs (NIIA).

Keshi joined the Nigerian Foreign Service in 1975. It has been an illustrious and accomplished career that has enabled him to serve in such outposts as Togo, Ethiopia, Belgium, The Netherlands, Namibia, and Sierra Leone. His tour of duty in the West African country of Sierra Leone lasted for about seven years, and left in him an indelible impression about the necessity for good governance, as well as the importance of fairness, justice, equity and development in Africa. He was among the diplomats who facilitated the Sierra Leonean Peace Agreement that set the pace for the resolution of the 10 year civil war in that country.

In his current assignment as Consul-General of Nigeria at the Atlanta Office of the Consulate General, Keshi oversees consulate services for most of the states in the South East of the U.S. Prior to coming to the U.S., he had headed a number of departments in Nigeria's Ministry of Foreign Affairs, including serving as an observer to Namibia's Constitutional Conference. While he has developed a keen interest in America and its politics, his forte, experience and career interest remain Africa affairs, negotiation, conflict resolution, and speech writing.

Keshi is a former soccer player and track and field athlete. His current hobbies include quash, tennis, golf, writing, listening to music, and discussing politics. He is married to Dayo Queenalia Keshi, and the couple has three children: Joseph, Jr.; Oluchukwu; and Nneka.

Portraits of Nigerians Who are Changing America

Honorable Joe Chinedu Keshi

Photo courtesy of the Office of the Nigerian Consulate General, Atlanta, Georgia

TAOFIQ OLAWALE OSENI

Consul General of Nigeria, New York, NY

Upon his arrival to New York as Consul General, The Honorable Taofiq Olawale Oseni revamped the New York office into an effective and efficient customer service-oriented diplomatic outpost for Nigeria. His assignment to New York was the latest in almost 25 years of service in Nigeria's Ministry of Foreign Affairs.

Born in Lagos, February 1, 1947, Oseni is the first child of Mr. Razaq Oladipo and Amunat Abike, both of whom are deceased. He has three siblings, and is married with four children.

Oseni's first arrival in the United States was in 1970, to attend Bowie State College, Bowie, Maryland. He graduated from the college in 1974 with a Bachelor's degree in Economics. He proceeded to Howard University in Washington, DC, from where he earned his Master's degree in Business Administration in 1976. Subsequently, he entered Nigeria's Foreign Service, motivated by his interest in International Affairs. He holds a Post Graduate Diploma in International Relations and Diplomacy from the prestigious Nigerian Institute of International Affairs (NIIA), Lagos. He is currently a member of the Institute.

CAREER DEVELOPMENTS

In almost twenty five years, Oseni has risen steadily from Third Secretary to his current position as Consul General in the Ministry of Foreign Affairs. Prior to his current assignment in New York, Oseni was the Head of the Liaison Office at the Nigerian Ministry of Foreign Affairs, in Lagos from 1996 to 1998. He served as the Special Assistant to the Honorable Minister of Foreign Affairs from 1993 to 1996, and as Minister Counselor in the ministry's Trade and Investment Department, from 1992 to 1993.

His other foreign assignments include stints at the Nigerian Embassy in Beijing, China (1977 to 1979), Permanent Mission of Nigeria in Geneva, Switzerland (1981 to 1984), and the Nigerian High Commission in Kingston, Jamaica (1988 to 1992), just to mention a few. He has been a member and/or has headed many Nigerian delegations to various international missions and meetings. He has also presented over a dozen papers, most of which deal with Nigeria's role in international relations, and policies issues during the tenures of some of the Ministers under whom he has served.

Portraits of Nigerians Who are Changing America

Honorable Taofiq O. Oseni

Photo courtesy of the Office of the Nigerian Consulate General, New York.

Tall Drums

Vice President Atiku Abubakar, GCON (center right) with the author, Ugorji. In the background, with finger raised, is Mr. Carlton Masters, President of Good Works International of Atlanta, Georgia. Good Works International co-sponsored the Quintessence Award ceremony in Trenton, New Jersey, on July 26, 2002.

Mrs. Jennifer Atiku Abubakar (right) accompanied her husband to the 2002 Quintessence Award ceremony. She is joined in this picture by Honorable Bonnie Watson Coleman (center), Chairwoman of the New Jersey Democratic Party, who was also honored with the Quintessence Award. Commissioner Gwendolyn Long Harris of the New Jersey Department of Human Services (left) co-chaired the event.

Portraits of Nigerians Who are Changing America

Part Two:

Sungai photo, 2000.

Featured Portraits...

ALASH'LE G. ABIMIKU, Ph.D.

While growing up in the hills of Jos in what is known as the Middle Belt of Nigeria, Dr. Alash'le Abimiku had no idea that she would be a warrior of international repute in the frantic global medical assault on Acquired Immune Deficiency Syndrome (AIDS). Now employed at the Institute of Human Virology at the University of Maryland, she is engaged in a trail-blazing international race to help develop a vaccine that does not just work, but one that would not leave the African continent behind in terms of AIDS prevention.

THE EARLY YEARS

Born on May 23, 1956 in Wamba, Plateau State, Abimiku is the fifth child of the late Mr. Abednigo Abimiku and Mrs. Mariyamu Abimiku. She has seven other sisters (one of which is now deceased) and two brothers. She attended the Roman Catholic Primary School in Muby, Adamawa State, and St. Louis College in Jos, Plateau State. In 1974, she entered the School of Basic Studies at Ahmadu Bello University, Zaria. After a year there, she enrolled in the University's Department of Medical Microbiology, from where she obtained a Bachelor's degree.

Looking back at her childhood, Abimiku recalls one particular thing among others. "Riding on horseback with my dad up the mountains of Mambila in Adamawa State, was quite memorable," she says. After her graduation from Ahmadu Bello University, Zaria, Abimiku left Nigeria in 1983 and went to London for her graduate education. She attended the London School of Hygiene and Tropical Medicines, from where she graduated with both a Master's degree and a Doctor of Philosophy degree in Medical Microbiology.

PERCEPTIONS

Abimiku had the perception that America was a land "where everyone drove a large comfortable American car," with authentic pairs of jeans to go with it. She looked forward, she says, "to a friendly but loud people, all of whom spoke the English language with a drawl like my White male chemistry teacher in Nigeria – he was well liked by all of us because of his cool way of teaching a rather difficult subject." After almost a decade in the U.S. Abimiku says her first shocker "was that not everyone could speak English," she says. "Yes, people are pretty friendly and love jeans. As long as you are willing to listen to

Portraits of Nigerians Who are Changing America

Alash'le G. Abimiku, Ph.D.

Tall Drums

their stories and laugh at their jokes, Americans really don't care whether you are from Mars," she adds.

MOTIVATION AND CAREER CHOICE

She arrived in the United States for the second time in December of 1990 as a postdoctoral guest researcher at the world-renowned National Institute of Health (NIH), in Bethesda, Maryland. She studied and worked in the frontiers of HIV and AIDS research under Dr. Robert Gallo, the co-discoverer of the HIV virus. Her choice of career in this area was sparked by the fact that "it was current and exciting," she says. She has observed that all the work on developing an AIDS vaccine have been done with subtypes from the industrialized world. "If those vaccines are effective in developing countries as well, that would be wonderful. But what if they are not?" she asks. "I wanted to be trained in this new epidemic so that I could be of help to Africa." According to Dr. Marc Bulterys, a medical epidemiologist at the NIH, "Abimiku plays an important role in bridging the gap between the developed and developing countries" in this research.

Abimiku met her husband, John Lorentze, here in the U.S. They first married at a church in Virginia, and then went to Jos, Nigeria for the African traditional wedding. John is from Denmark. On December 4, 1996, something she describes as her most memorable event in the U.S. happened to Abimiku: the birth of her and John's daughter, Sarah. "It was something," she recalls.

"Tell the truth, no matter what, and believe in yourself," are two of Abimiku's abiding principles. "No one has the right to take another person's life, and teach your children your culture," she instructs.

Portraits of Nigerians Who are Changing America

Strong and comfortable in her divinity, the Nigerian woman is just as active in the community as the man. Above, Attorney Ngozi Nwaneri moderates a ceremony at the Nigerian House, New York, 1995.

Photo courtesy of Sungai Corp., 1995.

CHINUA ACHEBE

Professor Chinua Achebe is Africa's best known writer-statesman. His works of fiction and non-fiction, now classics, have shaped both the consciousness of over three generations of Africans and the understanding of Africa by the rest of the world. The earliest pictures of traditional African life that Americans came to know were found on the pages of Achebe's books. The world of academe has recognized his historic contributions with over thirty honorary doctorate degrees. Nigeria has awarded him the Nigerian National Order of Merit, which is the nation's highest honor for intellectual accomplishment. He is currently the Charles Stevenson Professor of Languages and Literature at Bard College, New York.

THE EARLY YEARS

Born on November 16, 1930, in the village of Ogidi, Anambra State, Achebe is the fifth of his parent's six children. His elementary education commenced in Ogidi, and for his secondary education, he attended Government College, Umuahia, from where he graduated in 1948.

Achebe proceeded to the University College, Ibadan, and obtained a Bachelor of Arts degree (London) in 1953. Soon after graduation, he entered the field of mass communication and was appointed the first Director of External Broadcasting for Radio Nigeria, in 1961. By then he had already written *Things Fall Apart*, and *No Longer At Ease*, the first and second of what became the classic African trilogy. The third offering of the trilogy, *Arrow of God*, was first published in 1964. It was his fourth novel, *A Man of the People*, that thrust him into the contemporary Nigerian politics with its publication in 1966, just after the first military coup in Nigeria. Soon after, he left Radio Nigeria to serve in the Biafran Ministry of Information as war ensued between Nigeria and the short-lived nation of Biafra.

CAREER

Professor Achebe's career in academe started with his appointment as Senior Research Fellow at the University of Nigeria, Nsukka. He left Nigeria briefly to teach as Visiting Professor of English at the University of Massachusetts, Amherst (1972 to 1975) and from 1975 to 1976, he taught at the University of Connecticut, Storrs. He returned to the

Portraits of Nigerians Who are Changing America

Professor Chinua Achebe

University of Nigeria, Nsukka and retired rather early in 1981. The university named him Professor Emeritus in 1985. Other institutions he had taught at include Dartmouth College, City University of New York, The Anambra State University of Technology, Enugu, The University of Guelph, Canada, and The University of California, Los Angeles. In 1990, following an unfortunate automobile accident in Nigeria, Achebe returned to the United States to take up his current professorial position at Bard College.

Seeking a reconnection to a more glorious age of their culture, Nigerian groups in the U.S. have sought him as a guest of honor or as speaker at virtually all events of note in the community, and he has obliged as much as his physical restraints would allow. In 1999, he was named ambassador for UNICEF of the United Nations, at the recommendations of Ambassador Ibrahim Gambari of Nigeria. And in the same year, the Princeton-based Sungai Corporation honored him with its **Quintessence Award** for "Distinction in Letters and Outstanding Contributions to the History and Culture of African Peoples."

The writings and life of Achebe have become fields of studies in of themselves, with biographies written, and studies and interpretations of his works expounded. As an editor and publisher, his influence and mark were left on the African Writer's Series of Heinemann, London. He founded and edited *Okike: An African Journal of New Writing*, as well as *Uwa Ndi Igbo,* a bilingual journal of Igbo life and culture. His published books as an essayist include *Morning Yet On Creation Day; The Trouble with Nigeria*; and *Hopes and Impediments.* His book of poems, *Beware Soul Brother and Other Poems*, was published after the Nigeria/Biafra war, in 1972, and he edited a collection of Igbo Poems titled *Aka Weta*, in 1982.

Achebe is a foreign member of the American Academy of Arts and Letters, a Fellow of the Royal Society of Literature, London; and a Neil Gun Fellow of the Scottish Arts Council, to mention just a few. He is married to Dr. Christie Chinwe Achebe who has been a Professor of Psychology at Bard College since 1997. The couple are blessed with four adult children and two grandchildren.

Portraits of Nigerians Who are Changing America

Dr. Deforest "Buster" Soaries, the then New Jersey Secretary of State, congratulates Professor Achebe at the Quintessence Award ceremony in Princeton, New Jersey, 1999. Both men, along with Mayor Douglas Palmer of Trenton, New Jersey, were honored at the event.

Photo by Amaka Eze, 1999.

Ambassador Akunwafo (right) who is now Nigeria's Ambassador to Rome, congratulates Professor Achebe at the 1999 Quintessence Award ceremony. Standing next to Akunwafo are Professor Michael Mbabuike (center), and Dr. Ezegozie Eze (left).

VINCENT IRIVBUA AHONKHAI, M.D., FAAP.

His career in the pharmaceutical industry of the United States has put him in positions where he has contributed to and/or supervised the clinical development, registration, and commercialization of products that have yielded billions of dollars in sales. A soft spoken gentleman, Dr. Vincent Irivbua Ahonhkai has been credited with building efficient task teams not only in his medical and research professions, but also in the numerous civic and professional organizations to which he has generously lent his time and energy. He is currently the Vice President and Director at SmithKline Beecham Pharmaceuticals.

THE EARLY YEARS

Ahonkhai was born on December 22, 1944 to Mrs. Comfort Omejere Ahonkhai and the late Mr. Elijah Ojo Ahonkhai, at Sabongidda-Ora, Edo State. His elementary education took place at St. John's School in his village. His fondest childhood memory was his first trip to Ibadan as a passenger on a lorry: He had done well in the Common Entrance Examination (for entry into government secondary schools), and was invited to a scholarship interview at Ibadan. "I had never been out of my village, and I had never been in an automobile. The lorry ride was the most exciting and wondrous thing that had happened to me. To see paved roads, and street lights powered by electricity in Ibadan, left an indelible impression on me," he recalls.

His first five years at Edo Government College in Benin City, was on a Western Region Government Scholarship, while the subsequent two years of Higher School, at the same institution, was on a Shell-BP Scholarship. Ahonkhai held the position of Senior Prefect of the school during his last three years there. He was about to graduate when the Nigeria/Biafra war ensued. "It ushered in months of turmoil, and disrupted life and safety," he recalls. He proceeded to the University of Lagos to study medicine on a scholarship from Hamilton Goodwill Africa Foundation, and graduated in 1972. From 1972 to 1975, he was a Rotating Intern, Senior House Officer, and later Registrar, in pediatrics at the University of Lagos Teaching Hospital.

Vincent I. Ahonkhai, M.D.

PERCEPTIONS

Ahonkhai arrived in the U.S. as a medical resident in 1975 at the State University of New York (SUNY) Downstate Medical Center, Brooklyn, New York. "My original perception of the U.S. remains the same: It is a land of opportunity," he says. His favorite Americans include Martin Luther King, Jr., Basketball legend Magic Johnson, and the late actor Walter Mathau. "There is no more positive individual in my books than Magic Johnson," he says. Ahonkhai's most endearing hero, however, is his mother, Comfort.

He met and married Bernadine Ahonkhai at Lagos, in 1974. She is an educator who now holds a doctorate degree in the field. He says his most gratifying day in the U.S. was the day his wife joined him with their first child, Ebiho, who was born in Lagos. The couple has three other children, Aima, Omua, and Imoniri, all of whom were born in the U.S.

MOTIVATION AND CAREER CHOICE

Ahonkhai chose medicine because he wanted to "excel in the most respected and most challenging courses at the time, the sciences," he recalls. His training is in infectious diseases, and he completed a Fellowship in that specialty at SUNY Downstate Medical Center. He joined Merck Sharp & Dohme Research Laboratories, at West Point, Pennsylvania, as Associate Director in Clinical Research in 1982. He became Director of Clinical Research, Infectious Diseases in 1987. The Robert Wood Johnson Pharmaceutical Research Institute, a Johnson & Johnson outfit, lured Ahonkhai away in 1990, where he rose to become Executive Director.

SmithKline Beecham Pharmaceuticals recruited him in 1995. As Vice President and Director of Anti-Infectives & Biologicals, he is responsible for Clinical Research and Development and Medical Affairs for all of North America. Among the products which he has contributed to its development, registration and commercialization, is the highly prescribed Augmentin, SmithKline Beecham antibiotics for various bacterial infections. He has published over a score of articles, one chapter in a book, and lectured extensively in his field, throughout the world. "Doing unto others as I would have them do unto me," is Ahonkhai's abiding creed. He belongs to several professional and civic organizations, including the Nigeria Peoples Forum-USA, and he has received several awards for both his professional and civic services. He and his family reside in Lower Gwynedd, Pennsylvania.

Portraits of Nigerians Who are Changing America

Photo courtesy of Sungai Corp., 2000.

Like no other woman in the world, the Nigerian woman radiates elegance and style in a manner that is quintessentially African. Above, Mrs. (Lolo) Victoria Egwuonwu participates in a Sungai book launch. She is the wife of Chief Austin Egwuonwu, the former Chairman of World Igbo Congress, Inc. (the umbrella organization for the Igbo outside Nigeria).

BABATUNDE JUNAID AYENI, Ph.D.

As the U.S. successfully landed a man on the moon in 1969, Babatunde Junaid Ayeni was in Lagos, Nigeria, full of admiration for the technological and scientific accomplishments of the Americans. The sciences, he concluded, were where the excitement was. Ayeni has combined the disciplines of petroleum engineering and statistics to produce over 20 publications. His extensive works in the areas of experimental design and time series have produced models for oil production forecasting, crude oil reserves estimation, Bayesian estimation procedures for petroleum discoveries, as well as responsive surface models for minimizing product variability. The young man from Lagos has gone from admiring the technological feats of the Americans to contributing a few pages of his own to America's scientific annals.

THE EARLY YEARS

Born to the late Shittu Ayoade Ayeni (father) and the late Alhaja Lutifat Ayeni (nee Ottun), Dr. Babatunde Ayeni's remarkable life started at Isal-Eko in the early 1950s. The last of six children, Ayeni has two brothers and three sisters. He attended the Zumratul Islamiayah Elementary School, Lagos, from 1959 to 1967. "One of my most memorable experiences growing up in Lagos was the celebration of Nigeria's independence (from Britain) in 1960," Ayeni reminisces. "Every school killed big cows and we were all invited to eat as much as we could. An African giant had been born and her name was Nigeria," Ayeni recalls. He attended Ansarudeen Grammar School, Surulere, Lagos in 1968. In 1973, he transferred to Igbobi College, and later the Federal School of Science, also in Lagos.

Following the completion of his Higher Education diploma requirements, Ayeni had a brief stint as a clerical officer with the Nigerian Ports Authority. Armed with a scholarship from the Nigerian Federal Government, the budding scientist arrived at the University of Southwest Louisiana in Lafayette, Louisiana in 1976.

PERCEPTIONS

"I arrived through JFK (airport) in New York, and wondered how in the world I was going to survive for long in such a cold environment," Ayeni recalls about his earliest experiences in the United States. His marvel about America's technological feats, how-

Portraits of Nigerians Who are Changing America

Babatunde J. Ayeni, Ph.D.

ever, was heightened even more. In quick succession, Ayeni obtained a Bachelor of Science degree and a Master's degree in Petroleum Engineering. Eight years after leaving Nigeria, he earned a doctorate degree in Statistics.

Ayeni regards Dr. James LeBlanc, his former professor at the University of Southwestern Louisiana, as his favorite American. His other heroes include Professor Awojobi, formerly of Lagos University, Lawrence Omokachie, Paul Hamilton, and Muyiwa Oshode all former stars of Nigerian Green Eagles Soccer team.

MOTIVATION AND CAREER CHOICE

The scholarship he received from the Federal Government of Nigeria in 1974 was the major factor in Ayeni's choice of career. Upon the completion of his academic pursuits, he served as the Acting Director and Chairman of the Technology Department at Southern University at New Orleans. He is currently an advanced and highly sought after statistical specialist in the Information Technology Division of 3M Company in St. Paul, Minnesota. He has been with 3M since 1988.

At 3M company, Ayeni provides a variety of manufacturing, research and development divisions, and scientific laboratories with statistical and educational consulting. His achievements have helped 3M save over $15 million in costs over the years, and have won Ayeni several awards. Since 1994, he has been in charge of 3M's European Business, with responsibility for all statistically related projects and new products development.

Ayeni married his wife, Flora, in 1978, at Knoxville, Tennessee. He had met her in Lagos prior to arriving in the United States. The couple have five children – Abisola, Olarewaju, Adewale, Babatunde, and Olayinka. All five children were born in the United States.

Portraits of Nigerians Who are Changing America

His Excellency Governor Achike Udenwa of Imo State (one of 36 states in Nigeria) addresses an audience at Howard University, Washington, D.C., 2001. Photograph Courtesy of the Imo State Trade and Development Office, Washington, D.C.

CALLISTA O. CHUKWUNENYE, Ph.D., J.D.

Going to America had little appeal to her until her father told her that she could get her bachelor's degree in three years or less if she pushed herself. That was in 1976. Exactly three years later, not only did Dr. Callista Okwudiri Chukwunenye graduate with a Bachelor of Science in Chemistry, she did so *magna cum laude*. In a tribute to women in science, she was profiled, and her picture graced the cover of the April 1994 issue of the magazine for the *National Organization of Black Chemists and Chemical Engineers (NOBChE)*. Now, with a doctorate degree in chemistry, and a Juris Doctor, she is managing the FMC Chemicals Company's agricultural products registration and its regulatory affairs in North America.

THE EARLY YEARS

Chukwunenye is the second of the ten children of her father, Sonde Ahamefule Chukwunenye, from Owerre-Nkwoji in Imo State. Her father's job as a postmaster made her early childhood nomadic - each time he was assigned to open a new post office in any part of the country, he took his little girl with him. "I remember such things as crossing the Benue River on canoes with my father," she recalls of her childhood.

The last three years of Chukwnenye's elementary education took place at Holy Child Convent School, Ifuho, Ikote Ekpene, in Akwai Ibom State. For her secondary education, she enrolled at Cornelia Cornely College (CCC), Uyo. She was in her second year at CCC when the Nigeria/Biafra war ensued. "My education was interrupted for the three years of the war," she reports. "My parents lost their jobs. We literally started from scratch to make our first Nigerian Kobo after the war since the Biafran currency was no longer legal tender." She proceeded to finish her secondary education at St. Catherine's Secondary School, Nkwere in 1972. Two years later, at Queen of the Rosary College, Onitsha, she completed advanced level studies (Higher School) in the sciences.

PERCEPTIONS

In January of 1976, Chukwunenye arrived at Texas Southern University, Houston, Texas. "Everyone I knew who had returned to Nigeria from the U.S. painted a rosy picture," she recalls. But she would be shocked upon her initial arrival. "There were people here, including whites, worse off than most people in my extended family; in fact, worse

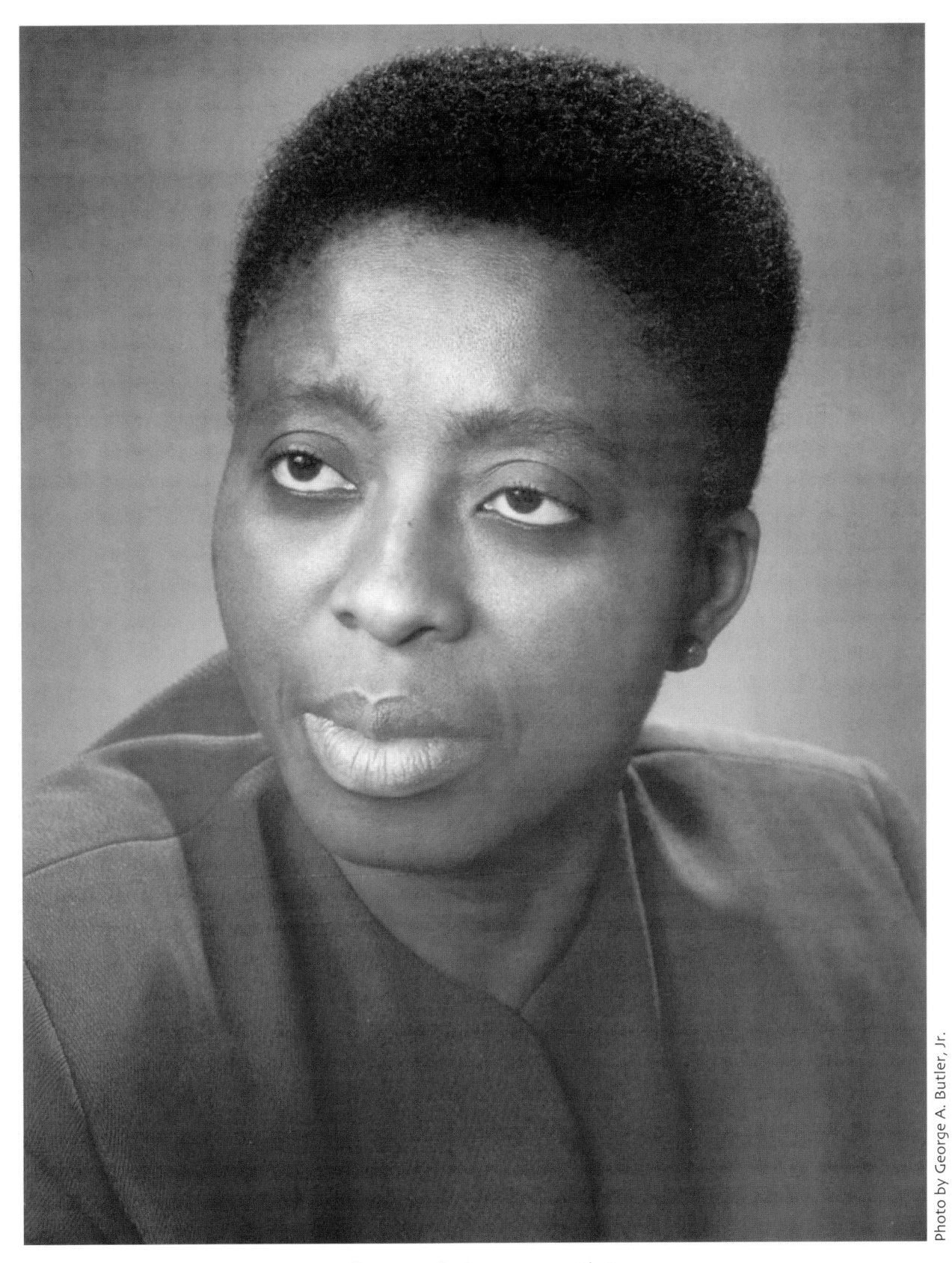

Portraits of Nigerians Who are Changing America

Callista O. Chukwunenye, Ph.D.

Photo by George A. Butler, Jr.

off than most Nigerians I knew. I just could not believe it." Her favorite American is the late trail-blazing politician, Barbara Jordan of Texas. She also remembers fondly two of her professors in college who encouraged her to pursue a terminal degree in chemistry – Dr. Bobby Wilson of Texas Southern University, and Dr. James L. McAtee of Baylor University, Waco Texas. However, she reserves the term "hero" only for the man who for so many years provided for, believed in, and pushed her – her late father. Philosophically, she believes strongly in both one supreme God, and a pantheon of "my noble ancestors."

MOTIVATION AND CAREER CHOICE

"My father always thought I should be a medical doctor," Chukwunenye reports. An "A" student throughout high school, Chukwunenye was particularly fond of chemistry. "There was something about chemical explosions, and watching colors change due to chemical reactions that was exciting," she recalls. "And I had this chemistry teacher who made the subject look like the coolest thing in the world." Her Bachelor's and Master's degrees in chemistry came in quick succession at Texas Southern University in 1979, and 1980 respectively. She went to Baylor University for her doctorate studies and graduated in 1986. She took a job with H.B. Fuller Company in St. Paul, Minnesota, as a Senior Chemist in 1986.

Chukwunenye enrolled in law school at William Mitchell College of Law, in St. Paul, while working full-time. She obtained her Juris Doctor in 1992, and a year later, the FMC Corporation in the state of Pennsylvania employed her as a Product Development and Registrations Manager. Her career focus shifted to Registrations and Regulatory Affairs for the Agricultural Group of the company. In her capacity as the main regulatory contact person between FMC and the US Environmental Protection Agency, she has shepherded the registration of the company's herbicides, and obtained registrations for several new crop uses and new application patterns for an existing insecticide. At the time of going to press, the company has split into two publicly traded, and independent companies: FMC Chemicals, and FMC Technology. Chukwunenye's visible role will remain with the Agricultural Group of FMC Chemicals. She resides and works in Philadelphia, PA.

Portraits of Nigerians Who are Changing America

Over 300 Nigerians attended the New Jersey reception in honor of Vice-President Atiku Abubakar (right) and his wife Jennifer Atiku Abubakar (center). Photographed with them is Ms. Chinwe Njoku (left).

Photo by Odinkemere

PIUS J. EGBELU, Ph.D.

The appointment of Dr. Pius J. Egbelu as the Program Director for Operations Research and Production Systems at the prestigious National Science Foundation in Washington, D.C., in 1994 was most gratifying. "For a recent immigrant such as me to be given such an opportunity at such an influential agency in the United States was overwhelming and humbling. It was beyond my imagination," Egbelu says. He has since moved on to become a full professor and the chairman in the Department of Industrial and Manufacturing Systems Engineering, Iowa State University, located in Ames, Iowa. It has been an extra-ordinary academic and professional journey for the young man from Ubeta-Ahoada, in Rivers State of Nigeria.

THE EARLY YEARS

The third of four surviving children, Egbelu is the son of Mr. Judah Egbelu and Mrs. Rozannah Egbelu. "I was born a Seventh-day Adventist, and that shaped my upbringing and childhood," Egbelu recalls. He graduated with distinction from the Seventh Day Adventist Elementary School at Ahoada in Rivers State. He attended the Western Ahoada County High School from where he graduated in 1973 with Grade One on the West African School Certificate. He arrived in the U.S. in 1974 and enrolled at Alabama A&M University, Huntsville, Alabama. He latter transferred to Louisiana Tech University.

In 1978, Egbelu graduated *Magna cum Laude,* from Louisiana Tech University with a Bachelor's degree in Industrial Engineering. He proceeded to Virginia Polytechnic Institute from where he obtained a Master's degree in the same field. Three years later, he obtained the terminal degree of Doctor of Philosophy in Industrial Engineering and Operations Research, also from Virginia Polytechnic Institute and the State University Blacksburg, Virginia.

PERCEPTIONS

Egbelu first entered the U.S. in August of 1974 to study the sciences. "I studied North America as one of my specialties in world geography while I was still in Nigeria." He was not disappointed when he arrived. "I was most impressed with the level of automation, industrialization, uninterrupted supply of water and other utilities, cleanliness of the

Portraits of Nigerians Who are Changing America

The author (right) introduces the then Nigerian Head of State and Commander-in-Chief of the Armed Forces, General Abdulsalam Abubaker (center) at a Sungai Book launching in New York, 1998.

PHILIP EMEAGWALI, Ph.D.

His school nickname of "Calculus" was prophetic for Dr. Philip Chukwura Emeagwali. His has been a push at the limits of computer technology, with ramifications in fields, such as modern weaponry, crude oil exploration, and information technology. In 1989, he received the prestigious Gordon Bell Prize, a highly coveted prize in the computer field - a prize which had hitherto been awarded to teams of professionals rather than one individual. Like Chike Obi before him, Emeagwali has emerged as an intellectual inspiration of legendary dimensions, who believes that African nations should skip industrialization and plunge into the information age.

THE EARLY YEARS

Emeagwali was born in Akure, Western Nigeria, on August 23, 1954, the first of nine sires of Mr. James Emeagwali and Mrs. Agatha Emeagwali. His family roots, however, are in Onitsha, Anambra State. "I spent my earliest years in Agbor, Delta State," he recalls. In 1960, he enrolled at St. Patrick Primary School, Sapele. His fondest memories were of the world boxing championship fights of Dick Tiger in Ibadan, and Nigeria/Ghana soccer matches. In 1966, he entered the St. Geroges Grammar School in Obiaruku. A year later, his family fled Agbor to the relative safety of Eastern Nigeria following the massacre of thousands of Igbo men, women and children in Northern Nigeria.

He was in his hometown of Onitsha when it fell to the Federal forces during the war. "I saw Nigerian soldiers shoot at women and children, and I saw rockets rain on the streets of Onitsha," Emeagwali remembers. The war and lack of finances caused Emeagwali to drop out of school thrice. He studied at home and earned his high school credentials by sitting for the General Certificate of Education (GCE) of the University of London, as well as the American Scholastic Aptitude Test (SAT).

PERCEPTIONS

Emeagwali arrived in the United States courtesy of a scholarship to Oregon State University in 1974. "I came to America for two reasons: Here I could work and go to school simultaneously. And because I wanted to become a scientist, I believed that America would provide me with the best opportunity," he says. In 1977, he earned a BS degree in math-

Portraits of Nigerians Who are Changing America

Phillip Emeagwali, Ph.D.

ematics, and proceeded to Georgetown University where he obtained two master's degrees in ocean and marine engineering, and civil engineering. He subsequently earned another master's degree in applied mathematics from the University of Maryland. His doctorate, in scientific computing, was completed at the University of Michigan, Ann Arbor. Among his favorite Americans are the Black mathematician Benjamin Bannekar, and Malcolm X.

MOTIVATION AND CAREER CHOICE

"My father was convinced that mathematics was a very important subject, and he set out to make me a prodigy," Emeagwali reports. "My early aptitude in mathematics influenced my choice of career in engineering and my use of supercomputers in problem solving. " Emeagwali uses multidisciplinary and unorthodox problem solving approaches that has reportedly resulted in about 41 inventions and discoveries, including the world's fastest computation of 3.1 billion calculations per second with a supercomputer in 1989. He has taken the concept of parallel processing in computer science to a new and potentially revolutionary level. The process involves the use of many computer processors at the same time to calculate or solve one problem. Using this process, Emeagwali simulated how oil can be recovered from oil fields with much more accuracy, thereby saving billions of dollars in oil exploration. The process can make weather predictions more accurate, enable three dimensional views of internal organs for doctors, and make internet sites astonishingly faster.

Emeagwali works as an independent consultant with various organizations, including the U.S. military. He is a highly sought visiting lecturer at many universities and institutes of technology through out the world. He has been inducted into the *The Hall of Fame of Who's Who in Computer Science*. His other accolades include the Nigeria Prize in 1997 for scholarly work, Pioneer of the Year by the National Society of Black Engineers, and numerous features in national and international publications. He is married to Dr. Dale Brown Emeagwali, a celebrated microbiologist in her own rights. They have one son, and reside in the State of Maryland.

Portraits of Nigerians Who are Changing America

"Drummers", a photograph by Olusegun Fayemi.

OLORUNTOYIN OMOYENI FALOLA, Ph.D.

Described by some as a premier authority in African History Studies, Dr. 'Toyin Omoyeni Falola is currently the Francis Higginbothom Nalle Centennial Professor of History at the University of Texas, Austin. He is at the head of the class of what has been described as the second generation of African history scholars whose works have broadened and deepened the field. His contributions to the documentation and teaching of contemporary history of African people has earned him not just awards, but a book on him, as a subject. Titled *"The transformations of Nigeria: Essays in honor of Toyin Falola,* the book was published in 2002 by Africa World Press.

THE EARLY YEARS

The last of nine children, Falola was born on January 1, 1953 in the historic city of Ibadan, western Nigeria. At the tender age of five months, he lost his father, James Adesina Falola, and later his mother, Grace Nihinlola Falola. His earliest years were spent in Ibadan where he attended Ibadan Public School, and the Okebadan High School, for primary and secondary education respectively. He was still in school when the Nigeria/Biafra war ensued. "Some of my friends and relations abandoned school to join the Nigerian Army," he recalls "a few brought back as wives women of Eastern Nigeria, thus creating enduring inter-ethnic relations."

In 1976, Falola graduated from the University of Ife with honors and a Bachelor's degree in History. He was subsequently admitted directly into a doctorate degree program at the same university, from which he graduated in 1981.

PERCEPTIONS

Falola's earliest perception of the U.S. was that the nation was the "world's capital of capitalism." He arrived for the first time in the U.S. in 1981 to give a series of public lectures, courtesy of the United States Education Travel Award. "People are friendly," he says of Americans. He names John and Diana Lamphear among his favorite Americans for their contributions to the development of Africa.

Portraits of Nigerians Who are Changing America

Oloruntoyin Falola, Ph.D.

MOTIVATION AND CHOICE OF CAREER

Early in school, Falola found a love for writing and chose to write and teach history. His research interest and specialization is in African history since the nineteenth century, with emphasis on West Africa, Nigeria, and the Yoruba speaking people. He has authored or co-authored over 35 books on subjects that deal with the economics, politics, transmission of knowledge, religion, military governments, and culture of African people. His articles in these areas have appeared in every respected journal in the field, and he has served as editor or associate editor of over a dozen such journals. Among his many notable works are *Nationalism and African intellectuals, Yoruba Gurus: Indegenious production of knowledge in Africa*, and *Violence in Nigeria: The Crisis of Religious Politics and Secular Ideologies*, to mention just three.

Falola's one abiding principle is intellectual honesty. He taught for over 12 years at the Obafemi Awolowo University (formerly the University of Ife) where he published a series of articles and books, trained a new generation of Nigerians, and administered academic associations. He left in 1991 and joined the Faculty of the University of Texas at Austin. He met his wife, Florence Olabisi Falola, in 1975, and they married in 1981. The couple has three children: Dolapo, Bisola, and Toyin, all of whom were born in Nigeria. He and his family currently reside in Austin, Texas.

Portraits of Nigerians Who are Changing America

Rubin "Hurricane" Carter is down for the count after receiving a devastating two-punch combination from Dick Tiger of Nigeria at New York Madison Square Gardens, May 20 1965.

ALFRED OLUSEGUN FAYEMI, MSC (Path) M.D., FCAP

Dr. Olusegun Fayemi's passion for photography and his recent publications of books in that genre have begun to change Americans. Fayemi prefers black-and-white photography. And his favorite subjects are African people – the less touched by Western and/or Arabic influences, the better for his lenses. But when he is not busy in the dark room, or when he is not in the company of some nomad guide somewhere in Africa taking pictures, he excels in the practice of medical pathology within the Bon Securs New Jersey Health System of New Jersey.

THE EARLY YEARS

Born on July 17, 1941 in Ifaki Ekiti, Ekiti State, Fayemi is the oldest of four children – he has two brothers and one sister. He attended Itesi Methodist Elementary School, Abeokuta, and Igbobi College in Yaba, Lagos State. While at Igbobi, he skipped a class due to academic excellence. He obtained his Higher School Certificate from Abeokuta Grammar School. The University of Ibadan, and the Hebrew University in Israel accepted him for medical studies. "I chose to go to Israel because the Israeli government at the time had offered scholarships for Nigerians to study medicine in Israel - five of us were picked. The World Health Organization later picked up the tab for our studies," Fayemi says.

Fayemi met another Nigerian named Ayodeji Bodunrin at the Hebrew University – Hadassah Medical School, to whom he got married in 1965. Ayodeji is a medical doctor with specialty in radiology. The couple has one daughter, Dr. Bamidele Fayemi Kammen. They also have two sons: Mr. Oluwole Fayemi, and Dr. Olutoyin Fayemi.

PERCEPTIONS

Fayemi arrived in the U.S. for the first time in 1970 to do residency in pathology at the Mount Sinai Hospital and Medical Center, in New York City. "I was already quite informed about the U.S. while I was in Israel. So, I knew it was a great place where there is both good and bad," Fayemi recalls. Once, when he traveled to Washington, DC by road, he was pleasantly surprised to see trees and national parks. "The country was not just bricks and steel after all," he recalls.

Portraits of Nigerians Who are Changing America

A. Olusegun Fayemi, M.D.

Fayemi says that the U.S. is now more like home. "When you come to consider a place home, you become kinder in your perceptions of the place. I've been able to work hard and live the American dream, and for that I am grateful," he says. One favorite American of his is President John F. Kennedy. He also admires "Hillary Clinton for her intelligence." Among his most favorite people in the world are Mahatma Ghandi, and Professor Adetokumbo Lucas, a former teacher of his.

MOTIVATION AND CAREER CHOICE

While he was in medical school in Israel, and after he had obtained a Master's degree in pathology, Fayemi became aware that there were very few pathologists in Nigeria. "That's why I chose to specialize in pathology," he says.

His interest in photography evolved over time. "I use cameras often in my work as a pathologist. And I have always liked to take photographs. Accidentally, I found myself in a dark room one day and saw images appear on a blank photographic paper, and I said 'wow!'" Fayemi remembers. That love for photographic images and his commitment to "present Africa to the world from the perspective of the African," has yielded two astonishing and widely acclaimed books, *Balancing Acts: Photographs from West Africa,* (Sungai Books) and *Voices From Within: Photographs of African Children* (Albofa Press).

His one abiding principle is simplicity. "I have never liked ostentatious living, and I believe in a divine presence in all of our lives," he asserts. Fayemi is currently the Director of Pathology and Laboratories of the Bon Secur New Jersey Health System. He also practices alternative medicine, and serves as both the Vice President of the Capital University of Integrative Medicine, in Washington, DC, and the Chairman of the institution's Pathology and Microbiology Department. He has authored and/or co-authored over 18 books in pathology and has written over 52 papers in the field. He also serves as a Clinical Associate Professor of Pathology at the Mt. Sinai School of Medicine, New York. He and his wife reside in White Plains, New York.

Portraits of Nigerians Who are Changing America

"A Playful Moment" One of the photographs by Dr. Olusegun Fayemi, first published in "Balancing Acts: Photographs From West Africa", by Sungai Books, 1994.

H. E. PROFESSOR IBRAHIM A. GAMBARI

Under-Secretary-General & Special Advisor on Africa, United Nations

His Excellency Professor Ibrahim Agboola Gambari holds a couple of records in the history of Nigeria's diplomatic mission. He was the longest serving Permanent Representative and Ambassador of Nigeria to the United Nations by the time he left Nigeria's Permanent Mission to the UN in 1999. He also holds the distinction of having served under six different Heads of State in that diplomatic position.

His had been a difficult task in service of country, during some of the most difficult years the Nigerian nation faced on the world stage. His loyalty was ultimately to his fatherland, good or bad. In 1999, he was appointed the United Nations Under-Secretary and Special Advisor on Africa, after Nigeria's return to democratic government.

Born on November 24, 1944 in Ilorin, Kwara State, Gambari attended Kings College, Lagos. He obtained his Bachelor's degree in Political Science, with a specialty in International Relations, from the London School of Economics. His Master's and Doctorate degrees were received from Columbia University, New York in 1970 and 1974 respectively. Both degrees were also in Political Science/International Relations. He plotted a career in academia, starting with teaching jobs at the City University of New York, and the State University of New York (Albany). Itching to return home, he obtained a teaching appointment at the Ahmadu Bello University (ABU), Zaria in 1977. He quickly rose from Senior Lecturer to Full Professor by 1983. As Chairman of the Department of Political Science at ABU, he established the first undergraduate Program in International Relations in Nigeria.

CAREER DEVELOPMENTS

Gambari's first foray into public service as a political appointee came in 1983 when he was appointed Director-General of the Nigerian Institute of International Affairs by the President Shehu Shagari administration. When the military struck later that same year, he was appointed the Minister of External Affairs. When that appointment ended in 1985, he returned to his natural habitat in academia, at Ahmadu Bello University. He served as a visiting professor at John Hopkins School of Advanced International Studies, in Baltimore, Maryland. He also had teaching stints at Georgetown University, and Howard University, and a Research Fellow position at

Portraits of Nigerians Who are Changing America

His Excellency Professor Ibrahim A. Gambari

the Brookings Institution, all in Washington, DC, from the period of 1986 to 1989.

During his tenure as Ambassador and Permanent Representative of Nigeria to the United Nations, Gambari served as President of the UN Security Council twice - May 1994, and October 1995. It was under his tenure as Chair of the UN Special Committee Against Apartheid that a new South Africa emerged, following the collapse of apartheid, a mission in which Nigeria had committed its resources for decades. He chaired the UN Special Committee on Peace-Keeping Operations from 1990 to 1999, and served as President of the Executive Board of UNICEF in 1999, as well as a Trustee of the United Nations Institute of Training and Research (UNITAR), from 1993 to 1999.

An accomplished and highly respected scholar, Gambari is the author of three books - *Theory and Reality in Foreign Policy Decision Making; Comparative Study of Regional Economic Integration: The Case of ECOWAS;* and *The Domestic Politics of Nigeria's Foreign Policy.* In 1999, he put together and edited *Nigeria at the United Nations Security Council, 1994 –1995 (Sungai Books, NJ),* and he is close to finishing two other books: *Africa's Security Questions at the End of the 20th Century Into the New Millenium,* and *The United Nations in a Changing World Order: An African Perspective.* He is the founder of the Savannah Centre for Diplomacy, Democracy and Development, a non-governmental think-tank in Abuja. The Savannah Centre will be devoted to critical analysis of conflicts prevention, management and resolutions, as well as the issue of sustainable development in Africa.

Gambari has been recognized widely for his accomplishments and services. In 1998, he became the first recipient of the **Quintessence Award** from the Princeton, New Jersey based Sungai Corporation, for "Outstanding accomplishments in international diplomacy and contributions to the history and heritage of African people."

Portraits of Nigerians Who are Changing America

Professor Gambari (right) being presented a proclamation from the Trenton City Council by then Councilman Nate Walker, during Quintessence Award ceremony, in 1998.

Professor Gambari (left) with the then Secretary General of the United Nations, Boutros B. Ghali (center), and the then Nigerian Minister for External Affairs, Major General Ike Nwachukwu (right).

JOSEPH NANVEN GARBA, CFR, fss

At the age of nine, General Joseph Nanven Garba knew he wanted to be a soldier. His father, a retired soldier, had fought at Burma during the Second World War in 1946 and imparted the military tradition in his young son. His career has taken him from the barracks to the highest diplomatic circles in the world. Some of the most glorious moments of Nigeria's prominence in international diplomacy took place while he was Nigeria's Minister for Foreign Affairs from 1975 to 1978. He now heads the Nigerian Institute for Policy and Strategic Studies (NIPSS) at Kuru, Plateau State, as its Director General.

THE EARLY YEARS

Born on July 17, 1943 in Langtang, Plateau State, Garba's father was the late Garba Miri-Wazhi, and his mother was Magwam Garba. He spent his earliest years in Langtang and later went to Shendam in Plateau to attend the Sacred Heart Primary School. "One of my earliest character traits was that I made friends easily across Nigeria's ethnic divides, particularly with the Southerners who lived in Langtang and Shendam," Garba recalls.

Upon graduation from the Military School at Zaria in 1961, Garba was admitted to what was known as the Military College, now the Nigerian Defense Academy (NDA). After the NDA, Garba proceeded to the MONS Officers Cadet School, Aldershot, England. At the age of 19, he became the youngest man to be commissioned as an officer in what was the Royal Nigeria Army, on November 2, 1962.

PERCEPTIONS

Prior to his initial visit in 1972, his perception was that the U.S. was just another United Kingdom. "I had had a lengthy experience in the UK, so I expected much of the same. What I saw was a huge expansive landmass. I was impressed by the huge skyscrapers in New York," he recalls. "The Americans have been very good to my family."

Among Garba's favorite Americans is Ambassador Jonathan Moore, who had a great influence in his life while he was at Harvard. He also mentions Oliver Johnson who came to Nigeria as a member of the Peace Corp in 1968 and has lived in the country ever since, coaching and popularizing the game of basketball all over the country. He also likes

Portraits of Nigerians Who are Changing America

Ambassador Joseph Nanven Garba

Former Secretary of State Cyrus Vance, Professor Jean Herskovitz of SUNY at Purchase, and President John F. Kennedy who he admired greatly.

MOTIVATION AND CAREER CHOICE

"There is perhaps no greater vocation, in which one demonstrates love for country than in soldiering," Garba says. Promoted to the rank of a Major General at the age of 36 in 1979, he became the youngest officer to be so honored. From 1978 to 1980 he served as the Commandant of the Nigerian Defense Academy, charged with the training of cadets who would become future generals, admirals, and air marshals in the armed forces of Nigeria. Following his military career, he was appointed a Fellow at the Institute of Politics and Center for International Affairs, Harvard University. He left with a Master's degree in Public Administration in 1983.

In 1984, Garba was appointed Nigeria Ambassador and Permanent Representative of Nigeria to the United Nations. He was elected the President of the United Nations 44th General Assembly in 1989, an accomplishment he regards as the crowning glory of his diplomatic career. In 1992, he was appointed a Consultant and a Senior Research Fellow at the Institute of International Education (IIE), in New York where he directed the IIE's South African Security Project.

Garba's honors include the Forces Service Star (fss), Commander of the Federal Republic of Nigeria (CFR), and two Doctor of Laws degrees from State University of New York at Purchase, and the Federal University of Technology, Owerri. In 1988, Harvard University recognized him with one of "Fifty World Problem Solvers Awards," and The Diplomatic World Bulletin declared him the "Diplomat of the Year" in 1990. The books he has authored are *Diplomatic Soldiering: The Conduct of Nigeria's Foreign Policy from 1975 to 1978, The Revolution in Nigeria: Another View, The Honour to Serve,* and *Fractured History: Elite Shifts and Policy Changes in Nigeria.*

Portraits of Nigerians Who are Changing America

Photo by Sungai Corp., 1995

Out of respect for Ambassador Garba, the Nigerian Nobel laureate, Professor Wole Soyinka, attended the New York launching of "Fractured History: Elite Shifts and Policy Changes in Nigeria," in 1995. Written by Garba, the book was published by Sungai Books.

JOHN KALU IJEM, M.D.

The legendary commercial town of Aba (now in Abia State) where Dr. John Kalu Ijem grew up, left its imprints in his consciousness. Almost two decades after he left Nigeria, Ijem's one abiding aspiration now is to use his success in the United States "to create a little bit of America in Nigeria." To that effect, he has readily supported every credible effort on the part of Nigerians in the U.S. to transfer both knowledge and financial resources to Africa's most populous nation.

THE EARLY YEARS

Born on October 28, 1956 to Mr. Sampson Ijem Orji and Mrs. Gladys Ogeri Ijem of Edda in Ebonyi State, Ijem is the oldest of eight children. "I remember the thrill of playing football (soccer) in the streets of that boisterous town (Aba)," Ijem recalls. He was still in elementary school when the war ensued. He left school to serve as an aide to wounded soldiers in a military hospital at Aba.

Following the war, Ijem returned to school and finished his primary education at Owutu Edda (now in Ebonyi State). He proceeded to Eziama High School, Aba, where he developed a love for the sciences, and became a soccer lord of repute. His first job after High School was as an aide in the psychiatric section of the prison at Aba. Later he tried his hands at sales with Benimo Enterprises, and at technical assistance for System Metal Industries, Calabar, an aluminum manufacturing plant. Soon, however, he decided that he had to go back to school.

PERCEPTIONS

"I had this notion that America was the land of opportunity, and even back then I was conscious that there were no guarantees," Ijem says of his earliest perception of the United States, prior to arrival in 1980. He obtained a Bachelor of Arts degree in Chemistry and the Natural Sciences from Midland Lutheran College in Freemont, Nebraska, and a Bachelor of Science in Pharmacy from Creighton University School of Pharmacy in Omaha, Nebraska. Only two weeks after walking away with his pharmacy diploma, he commenced studies at the University of Nebraska College of Medicine. And in 1990, Ijem accomplished a dream he had nursed at the bedsides of wounded Biafran soldiers: An American degree of Doctor of Medicine.

Portraits of Nigerians Who are Changing America

John Kalu Ijem, M.D.

"This is truly the promised land, but you must be creative, hardworking, law abiding, tax paying and God loving," Ijems says of the U.S. His favorite Americans include President Abraham Lincoln, President John F. Kennedy, Minister Malcolm X, and Dr. Martin Luther King, Jr. His hero is Dr. Nnamdi Azikiwe, the late founding father and first President of the Federal Republic of Nigeria.

MOTIVATION AND CAREER CHOICE

Ijem's interest in medicine was inspired by an experience his mother had during the birth of one of her children. "The care was so poor that even with our little expectations in Nigeria, I knew there had to be a way to care better for the ill," Ijem recalls. After medical school, he faced the choice of practicing as a general internist and pursuing a sub-specialty. "I was convinced during my cardiology elective rotation that cardiology was my calling. It is long hours, but the turning of almost hopeless situations into moments of hope and life give me an inner joy and satisfaction."

Ijem's goal is to become an expert in cardiac care, and his research interests are in all areas of preventive cardiology. "My studies would help in designing pharmacological treatments," he says. He has served as the Chief of Medical Staff, and Director of Cardiovascular Medicine/Chief of Cardiology at Grape Community Hospital, Hamburg, Iowa. And he owns a private practice in internal medicine and cardiology. In 2001, he joined Inlet Cardiopulmonary & Associates in South Carolina.

A founding member of the Association of Nigerian Physicians in the Americas (ANPA), Ijem is also Assistant Clinical Professor in the Department of Medicine at Creighton University School of Medicine in Omaha, Nebraska. He has two lovely children Whitney Gladys, and Bromley John.

Portraits of Nigerians Who are Changing America

One of the photographs by Dr. Olusegun Fayemi, first published in "Balancing Acts: Photographs From West Africa".

DR. MICHAEL C. MBABUIKE

Dr. Michael Chikeluo Mbabuike has designed courses that range from African Civilization and History to 20th Century Black Writers. He is a distinguished scholar and educator who has written and lectured extensively in the fields of anthropology, literature, social problems of minority communities in the US, and the African family. An ex-seminarian, he touches both the souls and the minds of future generations of not just African people, but also of non-Africans.

THE EARLY YEARS

Born on August 15, 1943, at Nimo, Anambra State, Mbabuike was the last of ten children, among who were seven males and three females. His parents, both of whom are deceased, were Okoye Alusi Mbabuike Nwasonuba, and Mgbankwo Mbabuike (nee Ezepue). He attended St. Patrick's Primary School, Ogbete in Enugu. For his secondary education, he attended All Hallows Seminary, Onitsha and taught at Christ the King College, Onitsha. "My fondest early memory is that of growing up and living according to the traditions of the Igbo, without any pretensions," he recalls. "Love and peace reigned and everyone was considered important. He returned to UNN after the war and earned his Bachelor's degree (with Honors) in Modern Languages in 1971. By 1975, he had earned both a Master's degree and a Doctorate degree in Literature and Anthropology from University of Sorbonne in Paris, France.

PERCEPTIONS

Mbabuike arrived in the United States in 1975 for professional purposes as a professor of literature and anthropology. He had the notion that America was "the land of democracy and opportunities. A great land of great people despite its racial relations flaws." Almost twenty-five years after his initial arrival, Mbabuike says, "My admiration and love for America remain intact. You can't but love the USA." His mentor, Professor Stanley Diamond, is perhaps Mbabuike's favorite American. Diamond was a professor of anthropology and a humanist at the New School of Social Research, New York. "And of course, Martin Luther King, Jr. was a man I admired very much," he adds.

Mbabuike met his wife, Christy Nkeiruka (nee Mgbako) first in Enugu in the 1960s. Their acquaintance was renewed when they met again in New York while she was a stu-

Professor Michael Mbabuike

dent at Mercy College. They got married in 1981 at a ceremony in New York. The couple have four children: Adanna, Nnenna, Obinna, and Onyebuchi.

MOTIVATION AND CAREER CHOICE

"The war (Nigeria/Biafra) conditioned and fashioned what I have become – a humanist," Mbabuike reveals. His first job in academe in the U.S. was at Seton Hall University, New Jersey. In 1976 he moved on to Fordham University in the Bronx, New York as an Assistant Professor in the Afro-American Studies and the English Departments. He served an unprecedented two terms as the President of the New York African Studies Association (NYASA) from 1993 to 1995. He has also lectured at Columbia University, as well as at New York University.

In 1986, Mbabuike was employed by the Humanities/Africana Studies Department of Hostos Community College, part of The City University of New York (CUNY) system. He founded and chairs the Alex Haley Lecture Series program. He was the chair of the College-wide Faculty Senate for six years, and chaired the Humanities/Africana Studies Department. A connoisseur of poetry and a published poet himself, he has authored five books and is a Trustees of the African Writers Endowment, Inc. He has established the Igbo Studies Center for Cultural, Literary and Language Studies at Hostos Community College, was made a full professor in 1994.

On matters of principle, Mbabuike insists that "the family is everything." An active organizer in the Nigerian community in New York, he says that there is nothing more important than the community. "I believe in knowing and loving your own people, and taking care of as many of them as you can. Sticking to and protecting my family is my abiding creed," he asserts. He and his family reside in White Plains, New York.

Portraits of Nigerians Who are Changing America

Professor Mbabuike (left) shares a humorous moment with Professor Achebe (right) in Princeton, New Jersey, during the 1999 Quintessence Award ceremony.

CHIKE "NNABUENYI" MOMAH

Chike Momah is credited with being a pioneer of a new genre of fiction, which Professor Michael Thelwell of the University of Massachusetts called "the Nigerian American novel." His first published novel, *Friends and Dreams* (Sungai Books, 1997) was described by Professor Chinua Achebe as a significant contribution to literature. In 1999, his second novel, *Titi, Biafran Maid in Geneva* (Sungai Books) was published. His third novel, *Like a Stream*, scheduled for publication in 2002, would continue in the "Nigerian American" genre and is expected to established him as the foremost teller to date of the Nigerian American story.

THE EARLY YEARS

Born on October 20, 1930, Momah is the second of the ten children of the late Sydney Momah and Grace Momah. Although the family's roots are in Nnewi, Anambra State, Momah was born in Owerre Nta, Abia State. Most of his elementary education took place at St. Michaels School, Aba. Upon graduation, he proceeded to Government College Umuahia for his secondary education. "I had a reasonably comfortable childhood," Momah recalls, "but Umuahia made me what I am and what I am not. There was order, discipline, and splendor in the environment. And the friendships that were formed there remained for life."

In 1949, Momah arrived at University College, Ibadan, with a crew of friends from Umuahia, including Chinua Achebe, Chukwuemeka Ike, Christopher Okigbo, and others. He majored in English, Religious Studies, and History, and graduated with a Bachelor of Arts (general) in 1953. While Achebe, Ike, and Okigbo embarked on writing and life in academe, Momah put his writing aspirations in the closet, intimidated, as he says, by the talents of his friends.

MOTIVATION AND CAREER CHOICE

Momah joined the Eastern Nigeria civil service in 1954 as a Land Officer. In 1956 he returned to the University College, Ibadan as an Assistant Librarian. From then on, he made library science his career choice. He attended the University College, London for one year to study library science, and obtained an Associate Diploma in the field in 1958. He returned to Ibadan and remained there until 1962 when Professor Eni Njoku took him

Portraits of Nigerians Who are Changing America

Chike Momah

and many others to begin his tenure as the first Vice Chancellor of the new University of Lagos. He proceeded to Paris in 1965 to study French at the Sorbonne. While there, he applied and received appointment as a librarian with the United Nations, in Geneva. After twelve years, he transferred to New York in 1978.

After his retirement in 1990, Momah opened the closet where his writing aspirations had been locked away. "I woke up. I decided to do what I should have done 30 years earlier. I aim only to write stories that people would enjoy reading," he says. The results have been the enriching of Africa's literary tradition, much to the applause of his more famous friends Acbebe, Ike, and others.

PERCEPTIONS

"One's earliest perception was that America was a land where milk and honey flowed, and it has turned out to be exactly that," Momah says. He arrived in the United States for the first time in 1976 as a visitor. Over twenty years later, he remains fond of "God's own country. When you live in a place, you see other things you don't care about, but it is a marvelous place," he opines. He names Martin Luther King, Jr. as one of his favorite Americans, on a list that includes President William Jefferson Clinton, Mayor David Dinkins of New York, and the Nobel Laureate Toni Morrison.

In 1959, he married his childhood friend, Ethel "Arunne" Momah, the daughter of the late Z.C. Obi of the Igbo Union fame. The wedding ceremony took place in Ibadan. The couple now resides in Somerset, New Jersey, and they have three adult children, Chukwudi, Adaora, and Azuka. In terms of principles, Momah says he has always striven to be honest, reasonable, and considerate of others.

Portraits of Nigerians Who are Changing America

A distinguished psychiatrist, Dr. (Iddi) Ambrose Mgbako is renowned in the New Jersey Nigerian Community for his philanthropy. Above, he speaks in his capacity as the Chairman of the ceremony during the launching of Chike Momah's second novel "Titi: Biafran Maid in Geneva," in Newark, New Jersey, 2001.

OBIOMA NNAEMEKA, Ph.D.

Professor Obioma Nnaemeka founded and heads the Association of African Women Scholars, and convened the First International Conference on "Women in Africa and the Africa Diaspora (WAAD): Bridges Across Activism and the Academy," in 1992, at the University of Nigeria, Nsukka. In 1998, the second WAAD conference on "Health and Human Rights" was held in Indianapolis, Indiana; it attracted delegations and participants from over 35 countries and 48 national and international organizations. The committed and socially conscious scholar's life now in academe is somewhat distant from the days in the late 1960s when, as a teenager with only high school French, she read the news in French for the Voice of Biafra. With endearment, her friends and colleagues still call her "Ici la Voix du Biafra."

THE EARLY YEARS

The third child among seven, Obioma hails from Agulu, Anambra State. She was born to devout Christian parents: Christopher Obidiegwu (deceased) and Jessie Obidiegwu. She attended the St. Bartholomew's Primary School, and later Queen's School, Enugu. She had just entered the University of Nigeria, Nsukka, when the Nigeria/Biafra war (1967 – 1970) ensued.

With just a high school French, Obioma was recruited to anchor the French news on Voice of Biafra. And each time the provincial capital of Biafra fell, she would move with the administrators to the next provincial capital. "During the war, my friends got nervous each time they saw me pack my bag. The radio station, Biafra's window to the world, was always the first to be evacuated whenever the town was threatened," Obioma recalls. At the end of the war, Obioma returned to the University of Nigeria and completed a Bachelor's degree with honors in French and German languages and literature.

PERCEPTIONS

Armed with a scholarship from the Federal Government of Nigeria in 1975 and a Junior Research Fellowship from the University of Nigeria, she arrived in the United States for the first time, to pursue graduate studies. "It was not my first encounter with the West. I had lived in Europe, and that transition probably mitigated the 'wow effect'," she

Portraits of Nigerians Who are Changing America

Professor Obioma Nnaemeka

recalls. In 1977, she graduated from the University of Minnesota, Minneapolis, with a Master's degree in French and African Studies. Later, she obtained a doctorate degree, also in French and African Studies, from the same university.

Obioma says her U.S. experience has been incredibly rewarding. "The availability of resources and the freedom to do intellectual work in the U.S. are rare," she says. Extolling the strength and pointing to the weakness of America, Obioma says the country has done exceedingly well economically and technologically, "but poor race relations remain the Achilles' heel of this great nation."

MOTIVATION AND CAREER CHOICE

"I actually excelled in mathematics and the biological sciences in high school and I was hoping to become a pharmacist," she recalls, "but as the best student in French in my class, I was offered a scholarship by my school to study French. That's how I ended up in languages." She now speaks and works in English, French, German, Spanish, and Igbo.

Obioma is a full Professor of French, Women's Studies and African American Studies at Indiana University, Indianapolis. "I wouldn't exchange what I am doing for anything else – using scholarship to effect social change, and bridging the gap between theory and practice," she asserts. She has taught at the University of Nigeria, Nsukka; the University of Minnesota, Minneapolis; and the College of Wooster in Ohio. An author of numerous articles and six books, she has received several grants from agencies and foundations. Her two books, *Sisterhood, Feminisms and Power: From Africa to the Diaspora (1998)*, and *The Politics of (M)othering: Womanhood, Identity, and Resistance in African Literature (1997)* have been best sellers.

"I can't stand restraints in any shape or form," she says. Her work is guided by what she calls the three Ps: Partnerships, Peace, and Progress. A member of the Board of many non-governmental organizations, magazines and scholarly journals, she has received many national and international awards, including the Distinguished Africanist Award, Daughter of Africa Award, Teaching Excellence Recognition Award, and Outstanding Faculty Award. She currently resides in Indianapolis, Indiana, with her children.

Portraits of Nigerians Who are Changing America

Dr. Gladys Nwosu (left) and her husband, Mr. Paul Nwosu, can almost always be seen at major Nigerian events in New Jersey.

Photo by Sungai Corp., 2000.

83

BARTHOLOMEW O. NNAJI, Ph.D.

Professor Barth Nnaji has made his mark in cutting edge industrial engineering, automation and robotics. And largely based on this merit, he was appointed the Minister of Science and Technology for the Federal Republic of Nigeria in 1993. More recently, he has embarked on establishing a credible and reliable voice for Nigerian Americans in the affairs of both the United States, and Nigeria. He has done this through the emerging Nigerian Peoples Forum (NPF-USA), which was founded in 1999, with him as its National Chairman. Adding to his list of honors, Nigeria has just recently honored him with the national award of Officer of the Order of the Niger.

THE EARLY YEARS

Nnaji is the first of 12 children of the late Mr. Emmanuel Nnaji Onovo. His mother, Nev Nnaji, gave birth to him on July 13, 1956, at Enugu. In 1966, he graduated (with distinction) from St. Anthony's Elementary School, Obe. He had admission to attend Government Secondary School, Port Harcourt when guns cried out in 1967 at the borders between Biafra, and Nigeria. He spent the next three years running to escape the fratricide. "Even when the war was declared over, and we returned home, I still witnessed executions of men and rapes of our women," Nnaji recalls. "Because we faced such tremendous challenges and survived, I am more resilient as a person. And I am more sensitive to my senses about Nigeria," he says.

Following the war, Nnaji enrolled at St. Patrick's Secondary School, Emene, in Enugu State and graduated in 1975. For two years after that, he worked for the East Central State Sports Council. He held the long jump title in the state and represented the state in national competitions. In 1977, he received simultaneous offers of scholarships from the Nigerian Government and St. John's University, New York to study Physics at St. John's, while the University of Nigeria Nsuka, offered him admission to study Mechanical Engineering.

PERCEPTIONS

"The magazines and books I read in high school painted a picture of America that was silver and gold," Nnaji says of his first impressions. "The first time I went to a supermarket here, I had this feeling that the store would run out of items," he remembers. "And I could not believe that one person could eat a whole chicken as a meal, as I saw Americans do,"

Professor Bart Nnaji

he reports. "If you work hard, you can achieve here; if not, you are going to be part of the dregs of society," Nnaji opines.

His favorite Americans are Presidents Bill Clinton, and Jimmy Carter, and the technology mogul, Bill Gates. "Under Clinton's leadership, the first Africa Trade bill that made sense was worked out. He insisted that Africa must be dealt with on trade basis, rather than on aid," Nnaji says. His other heroes include Nelson Mandela, Nnamdi Azikiwe, Chike Obi, Einstein, and Isaac Newton. "When I was inducted into the Nigerian Academy of Scientists, one of my honors was to see Professor Chike Obi present," Nnaji recalls.

MOTIVATION AND CAREER CHOICE

"I always wanted to be an engineer," Nnaji asserts. "I like reality. I like making things happen, and I like to build things." He graduated from St. John's University as the best student in his class in 1980 with a BS in physics. He proceeded to Virginia Polytechnic Institute and State University, from where he obtained MS and Ph.D. degrees in Industrial Engineering and Operations Research, in 1982 and 1983 respectively. His post-doctorate certification was earned at Massachusetts Institute of Technology in the field of robot manipulation, computer vision, and automated manufacturing.

Nnaji is currently the ALCOA Foundation Endowed Professor of Manufacturing Engineering, and Distinguished Professor of Industrial Engineering at the University of Pittsburgh, PA. He had taught at the University of Massachusetts, as well as directed the Automation and Robotics Laboratory there. He has served as Editor-in-Chief and Senior Editor for several journals in engineering, authoring over 100 refereed articles. He has over ten published books to his name, has supervised over 60 thesis in graduate studies, and served on scores of international bodies in various fields. Corporations have put up over $100 Million dollars to fund researches, with him as the principal or co-principal investigator. What he considers his greatest accomplishment, however, is the fact that he has helped "pay for the education of over 100 people at home."

Nnaji married Patricia in 1980, during a ceremony in New York. The couple met in 1979 when they were both students at St. John's University. They have two children, Chike Nnaji, and Nev Nnaji. Professor Bart Nnaji's abiding virtue is integrity.

Portraits of Nigerians Who are Changing America

The chairman of the North Jersey chapter of the Nigerian Peoples Forum, Chief Albert Ukaigwe is often at the forefront of organizing in the community.

Photo by Sungai Corp., 2000.

JOHN NWANGWU, MB, Ph.D.

Dr. John Nwangwu's profile is that of a scholar in academic medicine. He is currently a Professor in Infectious Disease and Epidemiology at Yale University School of Medicine, University of Connecticut School of Medicine, and Southern Connecticut State University. A Fellow of the American College of Epidemiology, as well as a fellow of the Royal Society of Medicine, he holds certifications in disease control, and tropical medicine. His work in this field has taken him to virtually every continent as a consultant for international bodies, including the United Nations.

THE EARLY YEARS

Born in Umuahia on April 16, 1952, Nwangwu hails from Ogidi, Anambra State. He is the third of six children of late Mr. Sydney Nwangwu, and Ms. Phoebe Nwangwu. His earliest years were spent in Umuahia, which is now the capital of Abia State. "I recall the year Nigeria gained its independence from Britain," he says, "we were all dressed up, and we ate and danced with joy." He attended St. Stephen's School, Umuahia, for his elementary education. He was in school at Government College, Umuahia in 1967 when the Nigeria/Biafra war ensued.

Nwangwu joined the medical unit of Biafra's Army. Following the war, he proceeded to Anglican Grammar School, also at Umuahia, where he completed his secondary education in 1972. He was at Government College Afikpo pursuing his Higher School Certificate when he received two offers for university education. Ahmadu Bello University, Zaria called, but he chose instead to go to Grace Bible College in Omaha, Nebraska. "Given the experience of the war, I felt it (the U.S.) would be a place of opportunity and deliverance for me," Nwangwu says.

PERCEPTIONS

Nwangwu arrived in the U.S. in 1973 to commence studies at Grace Bible College. Prior to his arrival he had expected to find superior students in his classes in the U.S. "I was surprised. I thought the students would be much better than I was, but I found the reverse to be the case," he reports. But he did find his place of opportunity. According to him "The U.S. has the best and the worst. It is a place for those who are disciplined and self-motivated, and those who know exactly what they want."

Portraits of Nigerians Who are Changing America

John Nwangwu, Ph.D.

Nwangwu names his late father as his number one hero. "A self-motivated and honest man," he says of his father, "I adored his discipline and ethics. He was very religious and hardworking." Dr. David Hendenson who spearheaded the global eradication of smallpox, is another hero of Nwangwu. "Dr. Henderson made a strong argument for epidemiology," he says.

MOTIVATIONS AND CAREER CHOICE

Nwangwu's stint with the medical unit of Biafra sparked his interest in infectious disease and epidiomology. "All I saw around me in Biafra was death due to starvation and infectious diseases. My memory of the sufferings influenced my choice of career," he asserts. He obtained his medical degree from the University of Nebraska College of Medicine, Omaha, in 1979. He proceeded to Loma Linda University, California, and completed a Master's degree program in Pubic Health in 1981. In 1988, he obtained a doctorate degree in Public Health from Columbia University School of Public Health, New York, and proceeded to complete a post-doctoral training in Clinical Epidemiolgy at Erasmus University Medical School, in Rotterdam, The Netherlands.

Nwangwu has made his marks in management of public health departments across the United States, as well as in faculty appointments held in some of the most prestigious institutions in the world, including Harvard University, and Yale University. He has written or co-authored over 65 refereed articles, and serves as a reviewer for a couple of professional journals. His other professional affiliations and honors include membership in International Epidemiological Association, Association of Teachers of Preventive Medicine, American Public Health Association, Connecticut Academy of Arts and Sciences, and New York Academy of Science, to mention a few.

Nwangwu's abiding creed is Christianity. "I won't go against anything I know for sure that God disapproves," he says. He met his wife, the then Chioma Nwokolo, while he was conducting research on Yellow Fever for the World Health Organization (WHO) in Bauchi, Nigeria, 1986. The couple married in 1988, in New York. They have three children: Nmadinobi, Tobenna, and Kamsiyochukwu. The family resides in Woodbridge, Connecticut.

Portraits of Nigerians Who are Changing America

Dr. Chika Onyeani (left) is referred to by the author (right) as the Dean of African newspaper publishers in the U.S.

DANIEL CHINEDU NWANKWO, M.D.

"The one good thing that came out of the war was that I met Ijeoma, my wife – I attribute most of my success in life to her," Dr. Daniel Chinedu Nwankwo said about the Nigeria/Biafra war. "Other than that, I was embittered at what happened to my people as the world looked away or collaborated." However, Nwankwo's sprawling medical practice in the Elgin and Carpentersville area of the State of Illinois is a far cry from his experiences as an infantry soldier with the Biafran forces. His skills as a specialist in obstetrics and gynecology and his good humor have been a comfort for thousands of families he has served since he started his practice in 1981.

THE EARLY YEARS

Born on January 10, 1947, in Enugu-Ukwu, Enugu State, Nwankwo is the last of six children of his father, Mr. Udezue Nwankwo, and his mother, Amoge Nwankwo (nee Okonkwo). He did his elementary studies at St. Theresa Catholic School, Enugu-Ukwu, St. Michael's Catholic School, Mina, and the Igbo Union School, Kano. He graduated with Division One in 1964 from Methodist College, Uzuakoli. He attended Government College, Afikpo from 1965 to 1966 and obtained the Higher School Certificate from University of Cambridge, and the Advanced General Certificate of Education (GCE) from London.

For a few months in 1967, Nwankwo taught Biology and Math at Isienu Community Grammar School. Then the war ensued in the middle of the year and he volunteered for the Biafran Army Infantry. He had reached the rank of Captain by the time the war ended in 1970. He had also met the woman who would change his life - he and the then Doris Ijeoma Osuoji married at Nkwerre two weeks before the war was declared over. The couple has four children: Amoge and Uchenna were born in Canada, while Teagbo and Chidera were born in the United States.

PERCEPTIONS

In 1971, Nwankwo departed Nigeria for Canada. He was admitted to Memorial University of Newfoundland, St. Johns for pre-medical studies and was subsequently admitted into Medical School without the requirement of a first degree. In 1976, he was awarded the Doctor of Medicine degree and proceeded to Calgary General Hospital for rotating

Daniel C. Nwankwo, M.D.

internship. He did his residency in Obstetrics and Gynecology at the University of Calgary Foothills Hospital.

"My first perception of the U.S. was that it was a land of opportunities. If you come and work hard, you will indeed succeed," he asserts. So in August of 1981, Nwankwo arrived in the United States and took residency in Elgin, Illinois. He has been in private practice ever since. He has served as chairman of obstetrics and gynecology at two of the hospitals to which he has been attached: Sherman Hospital, Elgin, and Provina St. Joseph's Hospital, also in Elgin. He counts Abraham Lincoln and Martin Luther King, Jr. as his two favorite Americans. But Nwankwo's living heroes are "the young Nigerians who have left the country to compete with the best in the world. Young men like you, Ugorji, make me feel less embittered and more hopeful," he opined.

MOTIVATION AND CAREER CHOICE

"When I was a kid in the village, I used to catch rats and attempt to operate on them. They died, of course, and I would cry my heart out," Nwankwo recalls about his earliest inclinations toward medicine. "And then there was this Texan eye doctor whom I had gone to see at the Sim Eye Hospital, Kano back in 1960. I was highly impressed with his craft and I remember telling him that I wanted to take his job. Medicine was always my love."

Regarding his beliefs, Nwankwo says the word "can't" is not in his vocabulary. "One must work hard and trust in God, that's the core of my principles." He also believes in giving back particularly to the little village he once helped defend during the war. He and his wife built a town hall for Umuatuora Village in Enugu-Ukwu. They also built the Pastor's House of St. Theresa Catholic Parish, also in Enugu-Ukwu, and the "Dan and Doris Habitat for Humanity," a home for indigent people in Umuatuora.

Portraits of Nigerians Who are Changing America

Chief Emmanuel Iwuanyanwu was one of the Nigeria Presidential Candidates who visited the U.S. (Newark, New Jersey) in 1998, seeking support.

Photo by Alex Iheke.

JAMES ESOMONU OBI

Described by *Class Magazine* as "The Third World's best salesman," Mr. James Esomonu Obi made his mark and fortune in the insurance industry. He fled Nigeria in December of 1966, following the second military coup, as the Igbo were hunted. Upon arrival in the U.S., he was driven to do better than just survive the pogrom. Through self-study and perseverance, he built and managed one of the largest insurance agencies in the U.S. during a thirty year period. He has been featured in such other periodicals as *The Enterprise Magazine, US News & World Report, Black Enterprise Magazine, Ebony Magazine*, and *USA Today* newspaper, to mention a few. Now retired, he owns the Obi Group, an investment firm with particular interest in profitable business ventures in Africa.

THE EARLY YEARS

Obi was born in Lagos to the late Mr. John Obi and the late Adannaya Obi from Ibele Umuaka, in Orlu senatorial zone, Imo State. The date was September 2, 1942, and he was the third son among the eight children of his father from her mother. His father had over 16 children. On his mother's side, he had three brothers and four sisters. He was only ten years old when his father, a civil servant with the Nigerian Railway Corporation, died in 1952. "After his death, I came to know poverty, because I grew up in it," he recalls. Raised by his mother, Obi and his siblings struggled to stay in school in Lagos and often could not, for lack of funds.

He decided early to become a businessman, and got involved in the export and import business, particularly in textiles. "I helped break the monopoly, which Lebanese in Nigeria held in the textile industry. We began to import directly from abroad with our own labels," he said. In the midst of the orgy of killing of the Igbo, which followed the second military coup in July of 1966, Obi says he had to leave Lagos for the U.S. after two attempts were made on his life. "I was in the U.S. when the war began. I did not believe that we were capable of killing each other in the Nigeria of that time; many of us thought it would not be long and we would all go back home. I lost all of my brothers in that war. I am the only surviving son of my father, and that was because I left," Obi reveals.

Portraits of Nigerians Who are Changing America

James Obi

PERCEPTIONS

Obi's arrival in the U.S. was in December of 1966. A Yoruba friend helped him with a passport because passports were not being issued to the Igbo at the time. He was able to get to the airport under an assumed name. Upon arrival he stayed at a YMCA in Manhattan, until another Yoruba friend, Sije Awosika, who was then at the Nigerian Mission to the United Nations, took him to share his apartment with him. "I came with only one suit, and it was cold in December. And I said to myself, 'here is a place one could accomplish anything.'"

Thirty six years later, he says America is a tough and demanding place. "It is a nation of opportunities, and it rewards you if you put in the effort. If you want to be good, you can be very good at what you do here, but if you want to fail, the nation can help you fail with flying colors," he says. Among Obi's favorite Americans is Mr. Reginald Lewis, whom he refers to as a brilliant entrepreneur. He also admires the entertainer Bill Cosby.

MOTIVATIONS AND CAREER CHOICE

The Ghanaian Joe Mensa got Obi interested in the insurance business. He considered himself then a seasoned salesman and figured that the insurance industry would provide him the challenge and opportunity he needed. "I did not know then why I was being turned down for employment by the insurance companies. I did not know that Blacks were just not welcome there, so I kept going to interviews." In 1967, he was able to convince a manager at the Equitable Life Assurance Society to take a chance with him as a Sales Representative and not pay him if he did not produce within three months. Ten months later or there about, he was made a District Sales Manager. Three years later, he was appointed as Agency Manager in New York, with the responsibility of building and developing his own agency organization.

By 1982, Obi's agency was number one in the U.S., and Equitable rewarded him with three President's Gold Trophies, and membership in the company's Order of Excalibur. Soon he became well known and highly respected in the insurance industry. He is a member of the Million Dollar Round Table, and belongs to the General Agents and Managers Conference. He has been awarded the National Management Award six times and the Master Agency Award twice. But his interests have gone beyond the insurance industry. He sits on the boards of several companies, including TLC Beatrice International Foods, Inc., The Glaucoma Trust Foundation, The Forum for World Affairs, and the Nigerian-American Alliance. He chairs the Board of Crescent Investment Group, Inc. He is a chartered financial consultant, as well as a chartered life underwriter

Obi met his wife, Cecilia Olubosede Obi (nee Oluwole) in 1962 in Lagos, and they married in 1964. Their first three children, Funke, Femi, and Sije, were born in Nigeria, while the fourth, Uche, was born in the US. All three sons and one daughter are adults now; they have made Obi a grandfather thrice and counting. He and his wife reside in Stamford, Connecticut.

Portraits of Nigerians Who are Changing America

Dr. Chudi Uwazurike is a scholar and playwright. He heads the Collin Powell Center at the City University of New York. His novel, "Yesterday Was Silent," was published by Sungai Books in 1994.

ELIZABETH ODILILE OFILI, M.D., M.P.H., F.A.C.C.

In 2000, the Association of Black Cardiologists in the U.S. named Dr. Elizabeth Odilile Ofili the President of its Board of Directors. Her election followed her appointment as Professor of Medicine and Chief of the Cardiology Section at Morehouse School of Medicine, in Atlanta, Georgia. She has received over $10 million in grants for over 25 research projects from various sources, including the National Institute of Health's Center of Clinical Research Excellence at the Morehouse School of Medicine, which she also heads, as Director and Principal Investigator.

THE EARLY YEARS

Born in Kano, on March 5, 1956, Ofili is the second of the seven children of Gregory Ebofuame Ofili and Felicia Nkedinma Ofili. The family hails from Ebu in Delta State. Her family later moved to Kaduna, where her father took up appointment with the U.S. information services. When the polgrom against the Igbo in Northern Nigeria began in 1966, she saw many of her Igbo friends begin to flee the North. "On one occasion, soldiers came to our residence with guns to ask for the Igbos; it was a frightening experience," she recalls.

As the war ensued, Ofili, her mother and her siblings were sent back to Ebu by her father. "There was a certain loss of innocence for me – I had to join my mother in the market as she took to commerce to make ends meet," she reports. She attended St. Theresa Catholic School at Ebu briefly, and returned to Queen Amina College in Kaduna where she completed her secondary education in 1972. She proceeded to Ahmadu Bello University, Zaria, in 1973 for pre-medical courses, and entered the university's Medical School in 1974. She obtained her medical degree in 1979, did her internship at the Ahmadu Bello University Hospital, Kaduna, and completed her obligatory one year National Youth Service with the Nigerian Air Force, also in Kaduna.

PERCEPTIONS

Ofili was fascinated by life in the United States. She arrived in the U.S. in 1982 for a Master's degree in Public Health at John Hopkins University, Maryland, which she completed in 1983. "When I arrived in Maryland, I was surprised at the segregation – everyone sat by themselves in the school cafeteria," she reports. Now, she says she has a clearer

Portraits of Nigerians Who are Changing America

Elizabeth O. Ofili, M.D.

understanding of the impact of race and racism. "I have a fuller appreciation of Black Americans, particularly in their model of how minorities can harness power in a democracy." Her favorite Americans are Martin Luther King, Jr., President John F. Kennedy, and President Bill Clinton.

MOTIVATIONS AND CAREER CHOICE

"It was respectable to be a physician. And because my mother was a nurse, I was surrounded by medicine," Ofili recalls. In 1986, she completed her residency in internal medicine at Oral Roberts University's City of Faith Medical and Research Center, Tulsa, Oklahoma. For her specialization in cardiology, she studied as a Fellow at Washington University, St. Louis, Missouri. She taught at St. Louis University, Missouri for a few years before joining the faculty of Morehouse in 1994. She has also served as a Visiting Professor at Harvard University, Cornell University, University of West Indies, Jamaica, and the University of Benin, Nigeria, to mention a few. She has authored or co-authored over one hundred articles and abstracts, written about ten books and/or chapters in books, and made almost two hundred presentations at conferences and lectures worldwide.

Ofili met her husband, Dr. Chamberlain Iheanyichukwu Obialor (from Mbano, Imo State) while they were at Ahmadu Bello University, Zaria. They married in 1984, at a ceremony in Tulsa, Oklahoma. Obialor is currently the Chief of Nephrology at Morehouse School of Medicine. They have four children: Chima, Sharon, Chinedu, and Nkechi. The family resides in Peachtree City, Georgia.

Portraits of Nigerians Who are Changing America

Photo by Sungai Corp., 2000.

The Quintessence Award ceremony draws some of the most distinguished people in the Nigeria community annually. Above, Dr. Ofunne Obaze (right), her husband Mr. Oseloka Obaze of the United Nations, Dr. Anthony Ihunnah of Rowan University, and Mr. Sonny Akpuda, former National President of the American Federation of Mbaise Associations (AFOMA), break bread at the 2000 Quintessence Ball.

HONORABLE EMMANUEL W. ONUNWOR

Mayor, City of East Cleveland, Ohio

In November of 1997, the Honorable Emmanuel W. Onunwor ushered in a significant new era in the history of contemporary Nigerian immigrants in the United States. Having served already as City Council President in the City of East Cleveland, Ohio, Onunwor challenged and defeated the incumbent mayor in 1997, thus becoming the first African-born mayor of an American city. And he accomplished this at a time when the image of Nigeria and Nigerians was at an all time low. The degree of competence and the community-oriented innovations the mayor has brought to his job, earned him over 70% of the votes cast in his re-election bid in 2001.

THE EARLY YEARS

Born in 1959 in the Umuomasi section of Port Harcourt, the capital of Rivers State, Onunwor attended elementary and secondary schools in Nigeria. He joined his older sister in the United States in 1980 to pursue higher education. He attended Cuyahoge Community College from where he graduated with an Associate degree. He proceeded to Cleveland State University where he majored in Urban Studies; he holds Bachelor's and Master's degrees in Urban Studies from the university.

CAREER DEVELOPMENTS

Onunwor's career in public administration began in 1985 when he served as an assistant planner with the City's Planning Commission. He later became the Deputy Project Director in the City of Cleveland's Division of Neighborhood Revitalization. In 1994, he left Cleveland to take up a job as the Executive Director of the East Cleveland Neighborhood Center. He was recruited to become the Director of Community Development for the City of East Cleveland, a Northeastern Ohio suburb of Cleveland.

Onunwor ran for and won a seat on the East Cleveland City Council in 1995. A year later, he was elected President of the Council by his colleagues. In 1997, he challenged the mayor who had recruited him to the city and defeated him during a rough campaign in which his Nigerian origin was made an issue. On January 1, 1998, he was sworn in as mayor, becoming the

Portraits of Nigerians Who are Changing America

Honorable Emmanuel Onunwor

third person to be elected mayor since the City of East Cleveland switched to Mayor/City Council system in 1984. Four years later, this trail blazing son of Ikwere was re-elected with over 70% of the vote in a city of 27,000 people. He doubles as the Safety Director of the City. As part of a significant reorganization of the City's Police Department, Onunwor appointed the first African American female Police Chief in the State of Ohio.

A member of both the U.S. Conference of Mayors, and the World Conference of Mayors, Onunwor serves as the Parliamentarian for the latter. He is a member of the Executive Board of the Cuyahoga County Mayors and Managers Association, and serves as the Associate Minister of East Mount Zion Missionary Baptist Church, in Cleveland, Ohio. Married to Pamela Randall Onunwor, the mayor has four children: Chinedu, Chinwe, Ovunda, and Ugochukwu.

Portraits of Nigerians Who are Changing America

A rising star in the Legal profession, Mr. Sebastian Ibezim, Jr. (left) is the Secretary to the Board of the African Writers Endowment, Inc. The lovely lady with him at the 2001 Quintessence Award ceremony is his wife, Pamela.

Photo by Marvin Ross.

CHARLES CHIBUIKE ONYIRIMBA, ESQ.

Within the legal profession in the Atlanta area, Charles Chibuike Onyirimba has made a name for himself as a consummate professional, with a policy not to handle divorce cases between Nigerians. In pursuit of his journalistic and entrepreneurial passions, he entered the world of newspaper publishing, with the widely-read monthly, *Africa Quest.* In 1996, the Nigerian Olympic Team arrived in the host city of Atlanta to a resounding reception and support system organized by Onyirimba and the Nigerian Olympic Reception Committee-USA, which he chaired. The Nigerian Team went on to win its first Gold medals ever – in the long jump, and in soccer.

THE EARLY YEARS

Born on May 16, 1961, Onyirimba is the third son of Sir Clifford Onyirimba, and Lady Mercy Onyirimba, of Ehime-Mbano, in Imo State. His parents had eight sons, and one daughter (the oldest son is deceased). He attended Central School in Ahiara, Mbaise, and Umueze Central School, in Ehime Mbano. For secondary education, he attended Madona High School in Etiti and graduated in 1978. He obtained his Higher School Certificate from Government College, Umuahia, in 1979. He worked for just one year as a clerk with the Mbano Local Government Headquarters before he left for the United States.

PERCEPTIONS

Onyirimba arrived in the United States in the Summer of 1981 for the sole purpose of furthering his education. "I had this picture of a well organized society, and I was not disappointed at all," he says. Three years after his arrival, he received a Bachelor's degree in Political Science and Journalism from the Oklahoma State University in Stillwater, Oklahoma. While at Oklahoma, Onyirimba served as the President of the African Students Association, President of the International Students Association, and Senator to the Student Government Association of the university.

He attended the University of Florida at Gainsville, Florida, from where he graduated with a Jurist Doctorate in 1987. He worked briefly for the Florida Department of Environmental Regulations before moving to Atlanta, Georgia in 1989. Onyirimba's views of America has not changed. In fact, he has come to appreciate even more the organized

Portraits of Nigerians Who are Changing America

Charles Chibuike Onyirimba, Esq.

state of the nation. He says his favorite American is Bishop T. D. Jakes of Potter's House, in Texas. And he names his father, Sir Clifford Onyirimba, as his hero.

MOTIVATION AND CAREER CHOICE

Onyirimba grew up knowing that he would either be a Bishop of his church or a lawyer. He chose the later, as he put it, "to further my sense of service to humanity based on my religious sense of right and wrong." He heads the law firm of Onyirimba & Associates based in Atlanta, Georgia, and is the President of the Urban Law Associates in Macon, Georgia. He is a member of the American Bar Association, the American Trial Lawyers Association, American Inns of Court Foundation, and the President of the African Lawyers Association of Georgia.

In 1997, Onyirimba founded Onyirimba Communications, Inc. and began publishing *The African Quest*. He is a member of the Boards of the African Trade Center in Atlanta, and the American-Nigerian International Chamber of Commerce, also in Atlanta. A founding member of the World Igbo Congress (WIC), he has served as the Chairman of WIC's Membership, Recruitment and Mobilization Committee, and Chairman of the Political Affairs Committee. During the second year of his term as President of the Igbo Union of Atlanta, he led the launching of a $1.5 million Igbo Cultural Center in Atlanta.

A community activist, Onyirimba's one abiding philosophy is "fairness and equity." He met his wife, Nkemdi, in the United States, and they married in a ceremony in Atlanta, Georgia in 1993. The couple has five children: Amuche, Dubem, Ebuka, Chidera, and Ezioma. All the children were born in the US. The family resides in the state of Georgia.

Mrs. Chioma Ugorji, 1996.

STEVE ADEKUNLE OSUNSAMI

Just this year, 2002, Steve Adekunle Osunsami was honored by Columbia University and The Ford Foundation for an impressive body of work in race and ethnic reporting for ABC's *World News Tonight with Peter Jennings*. It was only the latest recognition for a young man whose career as a journalist in America started just about a decade ago. As a News Correspondent with ABC News, his reports have also featured in *Good Morning America*, and the highly respected *Nightline* anchored by Ted Koppel. At only 31 years old, he is the youngest person profiled in this book.

THE EARLY YEARS

The first son of Olufemi and Margaret Osunsami, Steve Osunsami was born on February 6, 1971. He has four siblings - two male and two women (both of whom are older than him). His family hails from Lagos, Nigeria. Although he was born in Washington, D.C., he says his parents made sure that he and his siblings spoke fluent Yoruba at home. He attended Harrison Elementary School in Peoria, Illinois, from where he proceeded to Peoria High School. Upon graduation in 1988, he enrolled at the University of Illinois at Urbana/Champaign, Illinois.

CAREER CHOICE AND MOTIVATION

Osunsami graduated from the University of Illinois in 1992, with a Bachelor's degree in Communications/Broadcast Journalism. He was immediately hired by WREX-TV in Rockford, Illinois as Reporter and Anchor. In 1993, he moved to Grand Rapids, Michigan, where he accepted employment with WOOD-TV as a Reporter and Fill-in Anchor. After three years in Michigan, he worked as a Reporter for KOMO-TV in Seattle, Washington from 1996 to 1997. In 1997, he moved to ABC News and served first as a Correspondent for ABC News One. He now reports for *World News Tonight*, *Nightline*, and *Good Morning America*. He also serves as Substitute Anchor for *World News This Morning*, and *World News Now*, all at ABC News, and based in the Southeastern Bureau.

With interests in domestic issues and trends in the society, Osusami has reported on such cases as zero tolerance policies at American schools, those who spend years in jail for wrong convictions and yet get no financial assistance from the government upon release,

Portraits of Nigerians Who are Changing America

Steve Adekunle Osunsami

problems patients face with HMOs, and a controversial board game called "Life as a Black Man," which addresses, with humor, the trials and tribulations of Black men in America.

Apart from the Columbia University/Ford Foundation award, Osunsami has been recognized twice by the National Association of Black Journalists (NABJ), first in 1999 for a story he reported about Black Farmers on *World News Tonight*, and most recently in 2001 for a story about Black DNA, also on *World News Tonight*. In 2001, he was selected as a Finalist for the Livingston Award for Young Journalists, for a story about HMO Slow Pay. He was among the ABC News Millenium Coverage which received an Emmy Award in 2000 for Y2Kcoverage. His work at WOOD-TV of Michigan, an NBC affiliate, was recognized with awards from the Associated Press (AP) and from the Michigan Association of Broadcasters.

Osunsami resides in Atlanta, Georgia.

Portraits of Nigerians Who are Changing America

A recipient of the 2000 Quintessence Award, Professor Molefi Kete Asante is the most influential Black scholar alive today. Above, he welcomes guests in his capacity as the U.S. Chairman of the Board of African Writers Endowment, Inc., during Quintessence Ball, 2002.

JULIETTE MODUPE TUAKLI, M.D., M.P.H.

Dr. Juliette Modupe Tuakli speaks five world languages (Yoruba, Kiswahili, English, French, and Spanish). An advocate of the right of women to education and healthcare, her quest to learn and contribute to the body of knowledge in the medical field has taken her to virtually all the continents. She co-founded the African Health Initiative (a consortium of health and public health agencies dedicated to addressing health issues of African immigrants) and serves as a consultant to several healthcare institutions, including the World Health Organization. She is also the National Secretary General of the Nigerian Peoples Forum (NPF-USA). Her two daughters, who are currently seniors at Yale University, Connecticut, show promises of doing even better than their trail-blazing mother.

THE EARLY YEARS

Tuakli was the first of five children. Her father, Dr. Prince Akpabio from Calabar, Cross River State, is a dentist who works for the World Health Organization. Her mother is Mrs. Catherine Coker, from Abeokuta, Ogun State. She grew up in Abeokuta and remembers the rich cultural festivities of that historic city, including colorful masqueraded dancers. "There was this particular festival (Odun Oro) however, that I was not allowed to see. It took place only at night, and women were not allowed to watch or be part of it. I resented that very much," she recalls.

Some of Tuakli's elementary education took place in London, but she returned to Nigeria for high school. She attended the Abeokuta Girls Grammar School, and later transferred to Methodist Girls High School, in Yaba, Lagos. "I lost many friends to the civil war," she recalls, but her education was not interrupted. In 1970, she graduated from high school and proceeded to the Federal School of Science, Lagos. Upon graduation in 1972, she gained admission into the University of Lagos' Medical School, but chose to attend the St. Mary's Medical School in London instead.

MOTIVATION AND CAREER CHOICE

"I am told that when I was born, my maternal grandfather proclaimed that 'the healer in the family had been born.'" Tuakli reports. "Medicine affords me the autonomy to work for myself and participate in public service." In 1973, she got her BS degree from the

Portraits of Nigerians Who are Changing America

Juliette Modupe Tuakli, M.D.

University of Zambia. Three years later, she received dual medical degrees from the University of Zambia, in surgery, and medicine. In 1976, she obtained a medical license (L.R.C.P.) from the Royal College of Physicians, London, and became a Member of the Royal College of Surgeons (M.R.C.S.).

Tuakli's positions in academe have included Harvard Medical School where she served as a Clinical Instructor in Pediatrics from 1982 to 1999. She is currently in the faculty of the Boston University School of Medicine, and serves as a member of the Harvard School of Public Health Advisory Council. She has lectured extensively throughout the world, authored and/or co-authored several scholarly papers, and chapters in pediatric and child psychiatry books. In 1995, a United Nations special assembly gave her the World Citizen Award. And in 1999, the National Council of Negro Women recognized her for outstanding service in medicine. Her private practice received two awards for promoting cross-cultural childhood literacy in 2000, including the Well Child Institute Award from Blue Cross/Blue Shields.

PERCEPTIONS

Tuakli came to the United States as a Research Fellow in Maternal and Child Health at the University of California, Los Angeles (UCLA), California, in 1978. "My initial perception was that the US was a large, rich nation of kind people," she recalls. She did, in fact, find people to be very kind, but she had difficulty understanding "some strange behaviors on the part of some of my White colleagues. It took me a while to comprehend that the strange behaviors had something to do with my being Black," she says. Before leaving UCLA, she obtained a Master's degree in Public Health in 1979.

The legendary Paul Robeson who had traced his ancestry to Igboland, is Tuakli's favorite American. "He had to have been the most brilliant American ever. The man was phenomenal; he stood by what he believed in, and refused to be bought," she opines. Other American favorites of hers are the late W.E.B. DuBois, and Secretary of State Madeline Albright. She says her one abiding principle is "respect for fellow humans as children of one God." Tuakli's twin daughters, Eyi Taiwo, and Yetsa Kehinde were born in London in 1979. She met her husband, Dr. Kweku Ghartey of Ghana, at a Harvard Medical School event in 1982. They currently reside in Chestnut Hill, Massachusetts.

Portraits of Nigerians Who are Changing America

A distinguished inventor and Plastic Surgeon, Dr. Ferdinand Ofodile, and his wife, Carole, listen to presentations during a Sungai book launching in 2000. On September 28, 2002, Governor James McGreevey of New Jersey singled him out for recognition during the raising of the Nigerian flag, at the Governor's Mansion, to mark Nigeria's 42nd Independence Anniversary.

HENRIETTA NGOZI UKWU M.D., FACP

In national television advertisements run by the pharmaceutical industries of America, Dr. Henrietta Ngozi Chinyere Ukwu's face and words have extoled breakthroughs in pharmaceutical research and how the industry is changing the quality and longevity of life for all Americans. She has combined the gift of healing and scientific research skills in a manner that has made her uniquely experienced in Biologics and Pharmaceuticals. She is currently the Vice President, Worldwide Regulatory Affairs, Biologics/Vaccines at Merck Research Laboratories, Pennsylvania.

THE EARLY YEARS

Dr. Henrietta Ukwu's parents are the late Sir James Obiekezie Chibunze Ude, and Mrs. Theresa Udeaku Ude. Born on July 29, 1959 in Enugu, she is the second of nine children. She is nostalgic when she remembers times spent in her childhood in the "Coal City" of Enugu, with parents and her siblings.

In 1976, Henrietta entered the University of Jos, School of Medicine, in Plateau State, Nigeria. By 1982, she graduated with her medical and surgical degrees, and proceeded to the University of Nigeria Teaching Hospital at Nsukka for her rotational internship. It was during this time that she met her husband, Dr. Isaac Nwachukwu Ikechukwu Ukwu. The couple married in 1983.

PERCEPTIONS

Henrietta arrived in the United States in 1983 to pursue post-graduate training in medicine. "It's a beautiful and blessed nation," she opines of the US. "I was very impressed at the relatively large size of everything, the use of modern technology, and the diversity of the population," she says. Her favorite American is Dr. Edward Scolnick, President of Merck Research Laboratories, whose "ethics and brilliance in the application of scientific knowledge," she respects profoundly. She also admires the acclaimed neurosurgeon, Dr. Benjamin Carson, and she names Nelson Mandela as the epitome of "human compassion, wisdom, fairness, and truth."

Portraits of Nigerians Who are Changing America

Henrietta Ngozi Ukwu, M.D.

MOTIVATION AND CAREER CHOICE

"I chose medicine to touch human lives in a special way and to bring a spiritual presence in the healing of body and soul," Henrietta says about her career choice. She completed her internship in internal medicine at Meharry Hubbard Hospital, in Nashville, Tennessee in 1987, and her residency at the University of Tennessee Baptist Hospital, in 1989. From 1989 to 1991, she served as a Fellow in Infectious Disease at Vanderbilt University Medical Center, Nashville, Tennessee, where she also studied HIV/AIDS pathogenesis and worked on the development of potential HIV vaccines. She was subsequently appointed Chief of Infectious Diseases at the Alvin C. York Veterans Administration Hospital, in Murfreesboro, Tennessee.

Henrietta joined the Merck Research Laboratories in 1992 as Director for Regulatory Affairs, a position in which she was responsible for Live Virus Vaccines and Anti-infective agents. Important applications such as VARIVAX® PLA (a chickenpox vaccine) and CRIXIVAN® NDA (HIV protease inhibitor) were approved by the U.S. Food and Drugs Administration (FDA) under her regulatory watch and leadership. According to her, "The day the FDA approved CRIXIVAN® (in 1996) was the high point of my career so far. The clinical results were dramatic, and the HIV protease inhibitor provided immediate hope to the desperate situation of AIDS." In 1996, she became Senior Director and Head of Worldwide Regulatory Affairs for Vaccines/Biologics at Merck.

Henrietta is a Fellow of the American College of Physicians (FACP), and a member of several professional and scientific organizations, including the Association of Nigerian Physicians in America (ANPA). She has written and lectured extensively in her fields of expertise, and serves as Attending Physician for Infectious Diseases at the Veterans Administration Hospital in Philadelphia, Pennsylvania. She holds the chieftaincy title of *Ugochinyelu of Abor*, in Enugu State, as well as several professional and community service awards. She and her husband have three children: Nwachukwu, Nnennia, and Chinedu. The family resides in North Wales, Pennsylvania.

Portraits of Nigerians Who are Changing America

One of the rising stars in Nigerian politics, Honorable Godfrey Dikeocha is the Speaker of the Imo State House of Assembly. In September of 2002, he visited the United States and met with Imo State citizens.

Photo by Sungai Corp., 2002.

Tall Drums

INDEX

A

Abimiku, Alash,le, 16-18
Abiola, Moshood, xiv
Abubakar, Abdulsalami, 47
Abubakar, Atiku, xvi, 14, 35
Abubakar, Jennifer, 14, 35
Abulu, Toni, xiii
Achebe, Chinua, 9, 20-23, 76
Adeyemi, Yinka, xiii
Agbakoba, Olisa, xi
Agwunobi, John, xiii
Ahonkhai, Vincent, 24-26
Ajunwa, Chioma, xiii
Akinwande, Henry, xiii, 43
Aminu, Jibril, 2-5
Asante, Molefi Kete, xiv 115
Ayeni, Babatunde, 28-30
Azikiwe, Nnamdi, xi, 86

B

Biafra, xiv, 20, 32, 44, 52, 68, 74, 84, 88, 92,
Borke, Tim, xii
Bush, George W., 5

C

Carnegie Foundation for International Peace, xii
Chukwunenye, Callista, 32-34
Cosby, Bill, 98

D

Dick Tiger, xiii, 55
Dikeocha, Godfrey, 123
DuBois, W.E.B., 118

E

Egbe Omo Yoruba, xiii
Egbelu, Theopilus, 40-42
Egwuonwu, Austin and Victoria, 27
Emeagwali, Philip, xii, 48-50
Ezeife, Azubuike, 44-46

INDEX

F

Falola, Oloruntoyin, xiii, 52-54
Fayemi, Olusegun Alfred, 51, 56-59, 71
Fawehinmi, Gani, xi

G

Gambari, xvi, 60-63
Garba, Joseph, xiv, 64-67
Good Works International, LLC, 14

H

Harris, Gwendolyn Long, 14

I

Ibeabuchi, Ike, xiii
Ibezim Jr., Sebastian, 107
Ijem, John Kalu, 68-70
Ike, Chukwuemeka 76
Iwuanyanwu, Emmanuel, 95

K

Keshi, Joseph, 10-11
King Jr., Martin Luther, 26, 38, 46, 70, 72, 102

M

Mbabuike, Michael, 72-75
Mbagwu, Michael, xiii
Mbanefo, Arthur, 6-9
Mgbako, Ambrose, 9, 79
Momah, Chike, 76-79
Movement for the Survival of Ogoni People (MOSOP), xiii

N

Nigerians in the Diaspora Organization (NIDO), xiii
Nigerian Peoples Forum-USA, xiii, 26, 84, 116
Nnaemeka, Obioma, 80-90
Nnaji, Bart xiii, 84-86
Nwachukwu, Richard, xiii
Nwankwo, Daniel, xiv, 92-94
Nwaneri, Ngozi, 19
Nwangwu, Chido, xiii
Nwangwu, John, 88-90

INDEX

O

Obasanjo, Olusegun, 2
Obi, Chike, 48, 86
Obi, James, 96-98
Obioha, Tess, xiii
Ofili, Elizabeth, 100-102
Ofodile, Ferdinand, 119
Okigbo, Christopher, 76
Okoye, Christian, xiii
Okwu, Michael Chiaka, xiii
Olajunwa, Kakeem, xiii
Olanitekun, Folaside, xiii
Onyeani, Chika, xiii, 91
Onyirimba, Charles Chibuike, xiii, 108-110
Oseni, T., xvi, 12-13
Osunsami, Steve, xiii, 112-114

Q

Quintessence Award, xvi, 8, 14, 23, 62, 63, 75, 103, 107, 115

R

Robeson, Paul, 118

S

Soyinka, Wole 67
Sungai Corporation, xvi

T

Tuakli, Juliette Modupe, 116-118

U

Udenwa, Achike, 31
Ugorji, Stephen, 39
Ukwu, Henrietta, 120-122
Uwazurike, Chudi, xiii, 99

W

Watson-Coleman, Bonnie, 14
World Igbo Congress, Inc., xiii, 110

X

X, Malcom, 70

Z

Zumunta-USA, xiii